"The *General Directory for Catechesis in Plain English* is the latest evidence of Bill Huebsch's genius in making what seems complicated eminently accessible. Whether one is reluctant to delve into the GDC and needs a first taste, or one has read and studied the GDC and hungers for a deeper understanding, Huebsch provides. His writing is remarkably palatable, and yet is always solid food.

"Huebsch's reflective style enables his readers to mine the richness of the *General Directory for Catechesis,* drawn both by his poetic and practical presentation. As Huebsch writes in the Preface, this book does not replace the *General Directory for Catechesis.* Indeed, I found it offered further inspiration to my initial studies of the GDC; as well, it called me to return to the GDC yet again that its vision might be made real in my ministry."

Carole M. Eipers, D. Min.
Director, Office for Catechesis
Archdiocese of Chicago

"'Were not our hearts burning as he spoke to us along the way!' (Lk 24:32). No doubt about it, the disciples on the road to Emmaus had an unforgettable encounter with the risen Christ— one that the *General Directory for Catechesis* invites catechists today to share. In this new Commentary and Summary of the GDC, Bill Huebsch helps religious educators to rekindle the fire. His carefully constructed phrasing enables readers to experience the GDC in a prayerful, reflective manner. He makes it both accessible and inviting. I highly recommend this excellent resource to catechists, teachers, and DREs."

Gwen Costello

Au~~th~~   's

D1495243

"Reading Bill Huebsch's reflection on the *General Directory for Catechesis* makes one wish that all Church documents could be written in this way—simply, lovingly, and with a measure of eloquence. Bill does a great service to the Church he loves with his sense lines approach. I have used his "plain English" versions of the Documents of Vatican II with parish ministers in formation, and his style brings the text alive. Students who ordinarily would shrink from tackling a Church document engage with the text and discuss it with enthusiasm and even excitement. Bill has a deep commitment to the theology and aggiornamento of the Second Vatican Council and, indeed, his reflection on the GDC will be a fresh breeze in the catechetical world."

Jo McClure Rotunno
Religious Educator
Executive Editor, Benziger Publishing

BILL HUEBSCH

GDC

The General
Directory
for Catechesis
in plain
English

**A Summary
and Commentary**

TWENTY-THIRD PUBLICATIONS
A Division of Bayard MYSTIC, CT 06355

Fourth printing 2004

Twenty-Third Publications
A Division of Bayard
185 Willow Street
P.O. Box 180
Mystic, CT 06355
(860) 536-2611
(800) 321-0411

ISBN:1-58595-133-1
Library of Congress Catalog Card Number: 00-135776
Printed in the U.S.A.

Contents

Part One • Catechesis in the Church's Mission of Evangelization

Part Two • The Gospel Message

Part Three • The Art of Teaching the Faith

Part Four • Those to Be Catechized

Part Five • Catechesis in the Particular Church

Preface

I wrote this commentary and summary of the *General Directory for Catechesis* because I believe that everyone involved in this ministry should understand deeply what this wonderful document has to say. But Church documents can be hard to read and harder still to comprehend. Their language is often formal, and their footnotes often contain the Latin names of documents obscure to all but the informed few. Because reading them is so formidable a task, many people don't bother. Or those that do start to read, give up in frustration or boredom.

Many years ago, while I was working in the Diocese of New Ulm in rural Minnesota, I learned that it doesn't have to be that way. We can offer people another way to grasp the depth of Church teaching by way of texts such as the ones in this book. These texts are commentaries or reflections, article by article, on the General Directory offered along with a summary of the content of each article. When presented in this format, the text is no longer formidable. Now it virtually sings! It has a psalm-like quality, a modern psalm about the catechetical ministry of the people of God.

The GDC is presented here in summary form to assist pastors, catechetical leaders, and catechists themselves to more easily apprehend its content and meaning. The article numbers corresponding to the original document have been included to allow the user to move back and forth between the two, reading the original text and this commentary side by side. This is not meant in any way to replace the original texts of the GDC. It's meant to lead us to those original texts with new eyes and ears, with new interest and genuine faith, nothing more.

I invite you to use the study guide provided at the beginning of this book to work with others as you come to a deeper understanding of our ministry as catechists and catechetical leaders.

Bill Huebsch
Pine City, Minnesota

Study Guide for Use in Parishes and Schools

Introduction. Because this document is so important for the Church and its catechetical ministry, coming to know and understand it is very important. Here are some guidelines to assist you in grasping its content.

In your study, pay more attention in this Directory to parts one and two than to the balance of the work. The writers of the Directory themselves suggest that these two parts form the background for all Catholics around the world. But because all of us are in the ministry of catechesis, parts three, four, and five are also important for us as a practical matter and should not be completely ignored.

Whenever possible, work together with others in small groups or pairs to study these texts.

Step One. Begin by reading the text *out loud* in short sentences. In this summary form, the text flows prayerfully, almost like a psalm. By reading them out loud in a group, insights will arise and meditation-like reflections emerge that would otherwise not.

Step Two. Pause after reading it to allow the meaning of each section to sink deep into your heart and soul.

Step Three. Then share or journal together about what you have heard and felt. Identify what major ideas occurred to you while reading or listening. Use the following inventory to draw out your insights together.

Inventory.
What individual words struck you?
What memories of catechetical work did these texts summon for you?
What moment in a classroom or with your family came to mind?

What text of the *Catechism* or other spiritual work came to
mind?

What person did you remember or what personal experience in
your own life while you were being catechized?

What practical application do these texts suggest?

Most important, how do these texts inform and shape your
own experience of Christ?

Suggestion. From time to time, as the need arises, return from
this summary to the original text of the *Directory* to read and
meditate there, or to clarify particular thoughts and insights.

By gradual and prayerful study of these texts, catechists, direc-
tors, pastors, and even bishops will become more and more cen-
tered on the work of echoing the Faith in their own lives, and
by doing so, leading others to Christ.

Prayer for Groups Studying the General Directory

Before the study session begins:

Leader: My friends, we have been called to a ministry of catechesis in the Church. May we enter into this time of study with gratitude for this vocation and a desire to deepen our love for God and others.

All: In the name of God, Amen.

Leader: A reading from the Gospel of Mark

The reign of God is like a farmer who scatters seed in his or her field. The farmer sleeps and rises night after night and day after day. And the seed sprouts and grows, but the farmer does not know how or why. The earth produces of itself, first the blade, then the ear, then the full grain in the ear. But when the grain is ripe, at once the farmer cuts it down with his or her sickle, because the harvest has come.

Leader: This is the Gospel of the Lord.

All: Praise to you, Lord Jesus Christ!

Now begin your study.

When you are ready to conclude your study, conclude with this prayer:

Leader: O God, you have revealed yourself to us by the teaching and guidance of the Church, and by the words of Sacred Scripture.

All: Help us see you with clear eyes.

Leader: You call us to echo our faith to the world.

All: Guide us to do our work faithfully.

Leader: What we have seen and heard from you we now wish to share with others.

All: We go forth to tell everyone what we have seen and heard.

Leader: O God, we know that you are with us and you guide all we are about to do. Make us your worthy witnesses in a world starving for the nourishment of your word.

All: In the name of God, Amen.

The General Directory for Catechesis—in Plain English

Articles 1-13

Vatican II, in *The Decree on the Pastoral Office of Bishops in the Church,* called for the development of a directory which would guide the catechetical instruction of the Christian people. Here's what the Decree says,

> A special directory should also be compiled...for the catechetical instruction of the Christian people in which the fundamental principles of this instruction and its organization will be dealt with and the preparation of books relating to it. In the preparation of [this] directory, due consideration should be given to the views expressed both by the commissions and by the conciliar fathers. (*Decree on the Pastoral Office of Bishops in the Church,* article 44)

Indeed, such a directory was drawn up and published by Pope Paul VI on April 11, 1971. It was called the *General Catechetical Directory.*

During the period between the publication of that directory and the present one, some thirty years, a great movement for catechesis has arisen in the Church. Many dedicated women and men have come forth, generously contributing their time and talent, their vigor and deep faith, to build a catechetical enterprise around the world. Other forces also arose, forces that challenge the Church and the faith of its people. The Magisterium of the Church has watched all this carefully.

A series of important exhortations and instructions form the background for the present directory. They include,

• The Rite of Christian Initiation of Adults, published in 1972;

• the ongoing work of Pope Paul VI who considered Vatican II to be "the great catechism of modern times";

- the work of the General Assembly of the Synod of Bishops in 1974, whose work was published by Pope Paul VI under the title, *Evangelii Nuntiandi* in December, 1975;
- the first catechetical exhortation of Pope John Paul II, published in October 1979, *Catechesi Tradendae* which forms a cohesive unity with the work of Pope Paul VI;
- the twelve encyclicals of Pope John Paul II through which he enunciated the renewal of ecclesial life desired by Vatican II;
- various exhortations resulting from the ongoing work of the General Assembly of the Synod of Bishops, especially those which met in 1980 and 1987;
- the publication of the *Catechism of the Catholic Church* in 1992.

This new directory, the one you are reading now, has two main aims. First to place catechetical work in the context of evangelization, as envisioned by Pope Paul VI in *Evangelii Nuntiandi.* Second, to be sure the content of the faith is fully treated in catechetical work, as presented in the *Catechism of the Catholic Church.*

This directory is divided as follows:
- The introduction builds on the gospel parable of the sower and proposes guidelines for understanding human and Church conditions.
- Part One roots catechetical work in the Vatican II document on Revelation and places it in the context of evangelization as envisioned in *Evangelii Nuntiandi* and *Catechesi Tradendae.*
- Part Two sets forth norms and criteria for the work of catechesis, and also presents the *Catechism of the Catholic Church* as the reference point.
- Part Three discusses how we teach the faith.
- Part Four discusses the various groups of people being catechized.
- Part Five discusses the role of the local Church in catechesis, in particular the preparation of catechists.
- The Conclusion exhorts the Church to greater attention to the ministry of catechesis.

Note that parts one and two are more important than the balance of the *Directory*. Parts one and two have universal validity while the latter parts of the *Directory* are to be understood only as indications or guidelines.

The immediate aim of this *Directory* is to assist in composing local directories and catechisms. In places where catechesis and catechetical resources have reached a high standard, this document may seem insufficient in certain areas, while in less developed areas, it may seem excessive. Due note should be made while using it that not every local question or need is addressed here.

This document was published by the offices of the Vatican on August 15, 1997, with the approval of Pope John Paul II.

An article-by-article summary of the GDC

Introduction to the General Directory for Catechesis

Preaching the Gospel in the Contemporary World

Listen! A sower went out to sow (Mk 4:3)

[14]   We wish to foster in pastors and catechists
an awareness of the field
in which the seed is sown.

[15]   The gospels speak of a farmer who owns a field
in which he or she plants,
> tends,
> waters,
> and eventually reaps a harvest.

This gospel story is the basis for thinking about evangelization,
our first topic here.

Jesus is the first farmer.
> It is Christ who has sown a seed of faith
> > in our hearts
> > and that seed is the word of God.

Today Christ continues to plant that seed
> through the Church
> and the Holy Spirit.

And just as in the first century when this story was first told,
> some seed falls by the wayside,
> some on stony soil,
> and some among the weeds and thorns.

But some seed also falls *on good soil,*
> that is, among men and women
> who are open in their lives
> > to a personal relationship with Christ
> > and to solidarity with their neighbor.

My friends, the reign of God is near,

4

regardless the problems in the soil,
regardless the difficulties of the world.

The standpoint of faith

[16] Vatican II speaks of the joys and hopes,
the grief and anguish
of the people of our time.
These, the documents of the council tell us,
are the joys and hopes,
the grief and anguish
of the followers of Christ!
We Christians face the world in its reality,
but we see it through eyes of faith.
We know that every human event is laced
with the reality of God's creative goodness,
the reality of sin which limits and numbs us,
and the reality of power,
bursting forth from the resurrection of Christ
and filling the earth with new life!

The field that is the world

[17] And because we also see with sorrow
that so many people suffer today
around the world,
we wish to stir Christian hearts.
The presence of the Christian people (who are the Church)
can then be a sign of light and hope,
and the cause of justice will be served.

[18] Human beings have dignity,
and all human rights are rooted in that truth.
The Church (all the Christian people)
is concerned, therefore,
about the development of each human person
and of all peoples on earth.
We champion human rights
and reject whatever violates them,
including the right to life,

work,
education,
the forming of a family,
participation in public life,
and religious liberty.
[19] Where these rights are violated,
there is cultural and religious impoverishment,
which is on a par with material poverty
in its importance to us.
So the central task we undertake here
is to announce the Good News
which saves the world from all this impoverishment.
It is, in fact, the *only* way the world can be saved.
Catechesis has this as its ultimate goal!
[20] We are aware that "the seed" is sown
in a variety of cultures today,
especially the modern scientific culture
which is worldwide.
In this context, religious truth has a definite role
in unveiling mystery and love,
which science itself cannot do.
[21] There is also the desire to retain local cultures
in the midst of a growing worldwide web
of communication and interaction.
A satisfying human life is usually lived in a specific culture,
with its customs,
traditions,
and ancient connections.
We want to respect that and honor it and even encourage it
while at the same time announce the gospel clearly.
[22] There is a sense of religious indifference today,
a spread of atheism,
which is sometimes linked to science
as it tries to explain all things to us.
In the midst of this apparent atheism, however,
there is also a renewed interest in things divine,
sometimes expressed in emerging sects,
new religious movements,
and fundamentalism.

[23] There is also a moral challenge before us
        because many people today hold that there is
          no sure moral reference point.
As we proclaim God's word in the world, however,
      we provide people with a certain moral compass
          which is Christ's plan to save humankind
          through a deep bond with him.

The Church in the world

[24] Catechetical renewal in the Church in recent decades
        has helped give rise to Christians who
        experience God's mercy,
              who have rediscovered Christ,
              who have a sense of ministry in the world,
              and who are aware of the social obligations of faith.
[25] But there are also those who, although baptized,
        live as though they were not.
In these person's hearts, there is no religious feeling left.
There are also those of simple faith
        who follow popular devotions
        but do not understand their faith deeply enough.
There are also those adults
        who still live on their childhood lessons
        and now need to reexamine and develop their faith.
[26] And there are also, finally,
        those who shun an explicitly Christian life
        in favor of dialogue with others,
              secularism,
              or cultural pluralism.
A new evangelization is needed today in catechesis
        to address these situations more effectively.
[27] The inner life of the Church is key in this,
        especially the fruit borne by Vatican II
        and how it has been received in the Church.
Without doubt, liturgical life is richer.
        Indeed, more than ever before
              it is seen as the source and summit
              of the life of the Church.
The people of God understand better

that all share a common priesthood
founded on baptism
and lived with holiness and service.
The word of God holds a more central place.
And the Church's mission in the world
is now understood in terms of dialogue,
human development,
cultural diversity,
and the urgent quest for Christian unity.
[28] But all of this has also had its cost.
In some quarters the council has not been received well,
and in others, disagreement about its reforms
has led to divisions
which damage evangelization.
Because of this, we see it as urgent
that catechetical programs spring
from a unified vision of the Church as a communion.

Catechesis: Its successes and its challenges

[29] There have been recent great strides forward
in catechetical ministries.
Among these is certainly the large number of people
who now dedicate themselves full time
to this ministry.
Another is the rise of the catechumenal style
in catechesis
which leads to *formation* rather than merely *information*.
A third is the expanding role of adult catechesis.
And lastly, pastoral plans for catechetics are of higher quality
and richer content than ever before.

[30] But there are also some problems.
First, it's still not fully understood that catechesis
should be about being a disciple,
an apprentice in a *life of faith*.
Second, catechesis tends to focus on Revelation
more than it does Tradition.
But our two-thousand-year history as a Church
must be brought into play

even in order to understand Scripture properly.
Indeed, more balance is needed here.
Third, how we present Jesus Christ is sometimes
out of focus:
either too much emphasis on his divinity
or too much on his humanity.
Again, the answer lies in balance.
Fourth, certain problems exist regarding the content
of catechesis.
Doctrinal gaps concerning
the truth about God and humanity,
about sin and grace
and about the endtimes, is one.
The need for a more solid moral formation is another,
as well as more adequate treatment of Church history,
and more focus on social teachings.
Overall, texts tend to focus too much on selective interests.
Fifth, a weak and fragmentary link to liturgical life
often leads to a lack of attention to such things as
the liturgical year,
the symbols and rites of the Church,
and liturgical celebrations.
Sixth, over the years our method of teaching
has sometimes been in conflict with the content itself.
This doesn't have to be the case.
Good theological reflection
and good teaching can both be accomplished.
Seventh, we must work at proclaiming the gospel
in a variety of cultural settings
in such a way that it can really be seen as the Good News.
Eighth, there is not enough focus on the missions
of the Church in catechetical programs.

The sowing of the gospel

[31] God gives us the Spirit to guide us for this work
and also asks us to read the signs of the times
and be fully prepared.

[32] We must discover the presence and purpose of God

in today's events in the light of faith
so we can know the missionary needs of the day.

[33] The following challenges, then, are before us:
First, catechesis must present itself as a form of evangelization
    leading to missionary work.
Second, it must address itself to people of all ages.
Third, it must be based on ancient traditions
    and form people in faith, personality and all.
Fourth, it must announce the mystery of Christianity
    centered in the Trinity
    and leading to a life of faith.
And fifth, it must consider
        the preparation and formation of catechists
        a primary aim.

PART ONE

Catechesis in the Church's Mission of Evangelization

"Go into all the world and proclaim the good news to the whole creation."
(Mk 16:15)

The missionary mandate of Jesus

[34] After his resurrection,
    Jesus Christ sent the Spirit
    in the name of the Father,
    so that salvation might emerge from within
    and that he might animate his followers
        to continue the mission to the world.
Jesus was the first and foremost evangelizer,
    proclaiming the reign of God
    and calling it the gospel.
He made plain the joys, demands, and mysteries of this divine reign
    as well as a life of solidarity with others—
        all ending in eternal fulfillment.
[35] We are now going to treat catechesis in more detail.
First, we'll consider the theology of it all,
    especially as found in Vatican II's document on Revelation.
        This part will offer definitions and concepts.
Second, we'll situate catechesis within the work of evangelization
    and connect it to other forms
    of the ministries of the word of God.
And third, we'll analyze catechesis itself more directly,
    how it fits into the Church,
    how it must lead all to Christ,
    and how its style flows from the catechumenate.
We take all our concepts from recent documents,
    published mainly after Vatican II.
One's concept of catechesis, of course, profoundly influences
    how one approaches it
    which is why this is all so important.

Chapter One

Revelation and its transmission through evangelization

"Blessed be the God and Father of our Lord Jesus Christ...[for] he has made known to us the mystery of his will." (Eph 3:1–10)

God's providential plan is revealed to us

[36]   The fundamental starting point is this:
God, whose word creates and sustains everything,
offers us humans constant evidence of divine presence
through created things.
For our part, we, by our nature and vocation,
are able to perceive this
and to be certain of God's presence and power.
Revelation, Vatican II taught, is that act by which God
communicates God's own self to us
making us participants in the divine nature,
and thus, accomplishing God's plan of love.

[37]   This divine plan of God,
revealed in Christ
and realized in the power of the Spirit,
leads us to see
the true dignity of the human person,
the offer of God's grace to all people,
and the call to be the family of God.

[38]   God uses a teaching style or method
of making the divine heart present to us.
Hence, in the very words of Vatican II,
"...Revelation is realized by deeds and words,
which are intrinsically bound up with each other.
As a result, the works performed by God
in the history of salvation
show forth and bear out the doctrine and realities
signified by the words;
and the words, for their part,
proclaim the works,

and bring to light the mystery they contain."

(Constitution on Divine Revelation, article 2)

[39] Well, evangelization is also done
through words and works.
Catechesis transmits both, providing the proclamation
and also leading people to live by what they believe.
It recalls the marvels worked by God in the past
but also connects them to life today
where God's plan is now being realized.

Jesus Christ: mediator and fullness of Revelation

[40] Down through the ages, God has revealed himself
to us, culminating in Christ,
who completed and perfected Revelation.
Jesus Christ is God's own Son,
the final event among all the events of salvation history.
[41] Catechesis begins here:
it must show who Jesus Christ is,
his life and ministry,
and present Christian faith as the following of Christ.
Hence, catechesis must be based on the gospels.
In short, Christ is the center point of catechetical ministry.

The Church transmits Revelation through the Holy Spirit

[42] God wishes all people to be saved,
and to know the truth.
[43] To fulfill this aim,
Christ founded the Church
and gave the apostles the Holy Spirit.
The apostles then used words and deeds
to preach to the whole world.
The entire Church is responsible for continuing this work,
the pastors and all the faithful,
because the gospel is conserved whole and entire
within the Church itself.
And while the Church (all the faithful)
contemplates and meditates on this,
the Spirit continually causes the Church to grow.
[44] We can trust that the Revelation we have received is authentic

13

because it is carried through the centuries
by the Church's own teachers,
the Magisterium.
[45] Hence the Church is a sacrament of salvation,
announcing the Good News through the sacraments
and communicating the divine gifts to all.

Evangelization: the purpose of the Church
[46] Indeed, the very purpose of the Church
is to evangelize.
There are various aspects of this, which are all connected.
First there is the call to proclaim,
then to make disciples and teach,
then to witness to Christ personally,
then to baptize,
then to do this in memory of Christ,
and finally, to love one another in the process.
These are the means by which the gospel is passed on,
the means, in other words,
of evangelization.

The process of evangelization
[47] For its part, the Church evangelizes
through witness, dialogue, and presence in charity,
through proclamation of the gospel and the call to conversion,
through the catechumenate and Christian initiation,
and through the formation of community
by means of the sacraments and their ministers.
[48] Hence we might say the Church evangelizes
by renewing the whole world in charity,
by witnessing to Christ by the way we live,
by explicitly proclaiming the gospel and its call to conversion,
by initiating those who follow Christ into the community,
by constantly nourishing the faithful
through teaching,
celebrating sacraments,
and practicing charity,
and by arousing a sense of mission,
by word and deed,
throughout the world.

14

[49] Evangelization, then, varies based on its audience.
It occurs in "sacred moments" and unfolds slowly.
There is, first, missionary activity directed
toward non-believers
and those who live in religious indifference.
Then there is initial catechetical activity for those
who choose the gospel
or need to complete their initiation.
There is also pastoral activity directed toward
Christian people of mature faith
living within the community.
These moments flow together
and may be repeated
as the needs of each person and the community
call for it.
[50] In the ministry of the word
it is essential that
the name,
the teaching,
the life,
the promises,
the reign of God
and the mystery of Jesus, the Son of God,
be proclaimed explicitly.
They must be proclaimed to everyone,
including those already baptized.
The *words* used in this proclamation
must always point to the *works* of God,
to the witness of Christians,
and to the transformation of the world.
The human words used in this proclamation
are the means by which the Holy Spirit,
(who is the principal agent of evangelization)
does the divine work of salvation.

Functions and forms of the ministry of the word
[51] Here are the principal functions
of the ministry of the word:

15

First there is the call
        both to community and to faith.
This call is issued to non-believers,
        to those who have chosen unbelief,
        to Christians on the margins of the Faith,
        to those who follow other religions,
        and to the children of Christian families.
Second there is initiation.
This is how those who are moved by grace
        and decide to follow Jesus
        are introduced into the life of faith.
The work of catechesis is closely connected
        to the sacraments of initiation.
This work is done
        with nonbaptized adults,
        with baptized adults returning to their faith,
        with baptized adults not yet fully initiated,
        and with children and the young,
                who are really newcomers to the Faith.
Even Christian education in families and schools
        is initiatory in character.
Third is ongoing education in faith,
        sometimes called permanent catechesis.
It is intended for Christians already initiated
        but needing to nourish and deepen faith
        throughout their lives.
Fourth is the liturgical function.
The homily is a chief way this is accomplished,
        but celebrations of the word of God
        and sacramental instruction are other ways.
Above all is the participation of the faithful
        in the Eucharist
        which is the primary means of education
                in the Faith.
And finally, fifth is the theological function
        which involves the systematic treatment
        and scientific investigation of the truths
                of Faith.

[52] Sometimes these functions and forms
      occur together and in the same action,
      as when a homily is both a call to Faith
      and an instruction.

Conversion and faith

[53] In Mark 1:15, Jesus called us
      to "repent and believe the good news."
Today we speak of this as "conversion and faith";
      evangelization invites us to both.
Conversion is first. It is the full and sincere
      adherence to the person of Christ
      and the decision to walk in his footsteps.
Faith is a personal encounter with Jesus Christ,
      making oneself a disciple,
      and it demands a permanent commitment
            to think, judge, and live like him.
Toward this end, the believer is united
      to the community of disciples
      and takes on the faith of the Church.
[54] Coming to faith this way involves
      a twofold movement within the believer:
            trusting abandonment to God
            and assent to God's revelation.
This is possible only with the power of the Holy Spirit.
[55] And all of this, of course,
      demands a change of life,
      a *metanoia,* as it's sometimes called,
            on the part of the believer.
Our interior life of prayer and assent to God,
      our part in the mission of the Church,
      our married and family life,
      our professional life,
      and our part in economic and social work—
            all these are affected profoundly.
Thus everything we humans can hope for,
      everything that brings happiness,
      everything that fulfills the deepest human longing
            is all found in superabundance
            only in coming to faith.

17

Faith responds to the "waiting"
    which many of us experience
    even when we don't realize it.
We are waiting for the fresh water of the good news
    of Jesus Christ.
Faith, which is a gift, will be born in our hearts
    at the right moment.
Grace empowers us and we respond
    in complete freedom,
    turning our hearts toward God—
        and lo! Faith is born.
We venerate Mary because her response
    was lived so fully.

Continuing conversion

[56] Once we come to faith,
    continuing conversion is set in motion
    and lasts the rest of our lifetime.
Here again, several "moments" occur
    in this lifelong process.
First is an initial interest in the gospel,
    even without any firm decision.
This first movement of the Spirit
    provides an inclination to belief.

Second is conversion itself
    which occurs after a period of searching
    but is fundamental in the Christian life.
This "turning toward the face of God"
    leads to study, reflection, and prayer.

Third is the profession of faith.
Catechesis initiates the new believer
    in the knowledge and ways of faith,
    and a progressive change occurs
        until one is ready to profess one's faith fully.
There is both challenge and joy in this period.

Fourth is the journey toward perfection,
    the lifelong process of growth in faith,

moved by the Spirit,
empowered by the sacraments,
nourished by prayer,
lived in the practice of charity,
and assisted by ongoing education.
[57] The ministry of the word
is at the service of this process.

The religious situation of the world today

[58] There are three basic situations in today's world
which require careful consideration.
First, there is the situation of the non-baptized
where catechesis is directed mainly to young people and adults
and invites them to conversion.
The baptismal catechumenate is the usual form.

Second are communities possessed of a strong faith,
living a witness to the gospel
and made up of people with a profound Christian outlook.
In this, catechesis for children and young people
which helps them arrive at adulthood
with mature faith
is essential.

Third are so-called Christian lands
where, however, people have lost
a living sense of faith
or where Christian reference is purely exterior
to life.
These situations require a new evangelization
directed at the already-baptized.
[59] Now, these three situations
often coexist in the same city or neighborhood,
and certainly within the same nation.
The non-baptized mingle with the fervent,
while those who have lost faith
live together with those of great faith.
In a single pastoral setting, therefore,
all three forms of evangelization are needed
and they will influence, stimulate, and assist each other.

In order to achieve a proper balance
    these three principles must always be in play:
First, the primary task entrusted to the Church by Christ
    is the call of non-believers to faith.
We can never supplant it
with any other form of evangelization,
no matter how urgent.
Second, the model for all catechesis
    is the baptismal catechumenate
        which leads adults to a specific proclamation
            of faith.
This form should inspire all others
    both in their objectives and their dynamism.
Third, catechesis for adults must be considered
    the chief form of catechesis.
All other forms with other age groups
    are in some way oriented to it.
What is needed is a coherent catechetical program
    which meets local pastoral needs
    based on these principles.
Catechesis will then be situated in the context
    of evangelization
    and the missionary mandate of Jesus
        will be accomplished in the world.

Chapter Two

Catechesis in the process of evangelization

"[Apollos] had been instructed in the Way of the Lord; and he spoke with burning enthusiasm." (Acts 18:25)

[60] In this chapter we're going to consider
          three main points
          introduced by a fourth.
The first main point will deal with the connection
          between catechesis and sacraments of initiation.
The second will deal with catechesis
          in the ongoing life of the Church.
And the third will deal with catechesis
          in Catholic schools.
The introduction describes the relationship
          between catechesis
          and the primary proclamation of the gospel.
[61] Primary proclamation is addressed to nonbelievers
          and those living in religious indifference.
It proclaims the gospel and calls people to conversion.
Catechesis, on the other hand,
          promotes and matures initial conversion,
          educates the one converted,
          and incorporates him or her into the community.
These two activities are distinct from one another
          yet complement each other,
          and every Christian is called to both.
[62] However, their boundaries are not always easily defined
          in actual pastoral practice.
Many who present themselves for catechesis, for example,
          are actually in need of the call to conversion.
Therefore, the first stage of catechetical ministry
          should usually be dedicated to ensuring conversion.
This might take the form of the pre-catechumenate
          or a period of introduction to the Lord
          where the learner first meets Christ.

Let it be understood, however, that beginning catechesis
by a call to conversion
does not dispense a parish from also
having a program of primary proclamation
which is Jesus' direct command to us.

Catechesis and Christian initiation

[63] There are activities which prepare people for catechesis,
and activities which derive from catechesis.
The moment of catechesis itself falls between these.
It is that moment in which conversion to Christ is formalized
and which provides a basis for deepening faith in him.
[64] Hence, catechesis lays the foundation
for building a life of faith.
It is the link between primary proclamation
which prepares people for it
and pastoral activity which flows from it.
It's essential and fundamental and must always be a priority.
[65] Christ commanded that his followers do two things:
make disciples of all nations
and baptize them.
Hence, the mission to baptize is integrally connected
to the work of evangelization
and to the catechesis which is part of that work.
This is how the sacraments of initiation function
(baptism/confirmation and Eucharist):
they provide the ones initiated
with the tools for a life of faith in Christ.
[66] In fact, the goal of catechesis is precisely this:
to encourage a living, explicit, and fruitful
profession of faith.
For this reason, catechetical work is essential to initiation
because in catechesis the Church transmits
her living experience of the gospel (her faith)
so the newcomers may make it their own
and profess it.
In the words of an Apostolic Exhortation
from Pope John Paul II,

called in Latin *Catechesi Tradendae*
and published in October, 1979,
        "Authentic catechesis is always
            an orderly and systematic initiation
            into the revelation that God has given
                of himself
                to humanity
                in Christ Jesus,
            a revelation stored in the depths
            of the Church's memory and Sacred Scripture,
                and constantly communicated
                from one generation to the next
                by a living active tradition."
[67] It flows from this that catechesis
        has certain identifying characteristics.
First, it is always *comprehensive and systematic*
        which distinguishes it from other forms
        of presenting the word of God, such as homilies.
Second, it is more than mere instruction.
        It is *an apprenticeship* of the entire Christian life
            which is focused on the person of Jesus Christ.
        When it passes on knowledge,
            it does so only to help the apprentice
            feel enriched by the word of God
                at his or her deepest level.
And third, it is a basic and essential *formation*,
        focused on central realities of faith
        and laying the foundation for a life of faith
            in the ordinary flow of the Christian community.
[68] In sum,
        catechesis is not accidental
        but well-planned and comprehensive.
                It is more than mere instruction.
It looks for what is common in the Christian life
        and avoids disputed questions
        and theological investigation.
And finally, it incorporates people into the community
        and it is the model for all catechesis.

Catechesis at the service of ongoing formation in the faith

[69] Once a person has experienced the initial catechesis
which follows on his or her conversion,
ongoing formation in faith is essential.
In order for it to happen,
the newly formed must be welcomed by a community
ready to sustain and deepen their experience.

[70] In this Christian community,
the twofold table of Eucharist and word
is where nourishment is found.
Here both the gift of communion
and the task of mission
are deepened and lived
in an increasingly intense way.
Jesus prayed that we might be one
so those who see us see Christ in us.
Living as a community of word and Eucharist
has this as its outcome: unity in Christ
by the power of the Holy Spirit.
In this process the homily is important
as a means of catechesis
because it encourages the community to live
each day as a spiritual journey to the heart of the Lord.

[71] There are various forms of continuing catechesis.
First there is the study of Scripture,
read with the Church and her living faith
in such a way as to arouse a response of faith.
The Liturgy of the Hours is a fine way to do this.
Second, there is the study of the social teaching
of the Church
which allows us to understand world events
through the lens of Christian understanding.
Third, there is liturgical catechesis
which helps people understand more fully
the meaning of the signs and symbols,
the prayers and gestures,
the role of participation and that of silence.
Fourth, there is a form of catechesis

through which the circumstances of life
are understood in the light of faith.
Fifth, there is spiritual direction and other forms
of intentional growth in faith or prayer.
Sixth, there is theological instruction
which allows a learner to undertake
a systematic study of the faith.
[72] It's very important that initial catechesis
with its systematic and comprehensive approach,
and ongoing catechesis with its variety of forms,
be closely linked
with the whole community
to promote harmony and authenticity.
Likewise, catechesis of children and that of adults
should be complementary and connected.

Catechesis and religious instruction in schools

[73] It is necessary to distinguish between
religious instruction on one hand
and catechesis on the other,
especially as it's experienced in Catholic schools.
Religious instruction in schools
should be handled just as any other course is handled,
and should not be considered a "less important" subject.
It should have the same systematic demands
and the same rigor as other disciplines.
It should, in fact, lead to a dialogue
among disciplines
which allows students to understand everything
in light of their faith, including
the origins of the world,
the events of history,
the basis of ethical values,
the place of religion in culture,
the destiny of the human race,
and our relationship with nature.
[74] In some nations,
religious instruction of this sort
happens in public schools,

and when it does
it should not be compromised.
Within the Catholic school it should be part
of a wider program of formation
including catechesis, homilies, and liturgies.
[75] Religious instructors should be aware of
the constantly changing environment
in which their students live.
For believers, religious instruction helps them
see their faith as part of the great search
undertaken by humans for truth.
For searchers, such instruction gives them the possibility
of choosing Christ.
And for non-believers, such instruction
serves as initial proclamation
and may lead them to decide for the faith.
[76] Each episcopal conference should establish guidelines
regarding formation
in the family,
the parish,
and the school.

Chapter Three

The nature, object, and duties of catechesis

"Every tongue should confess that Jesus Christ is Lord." (Phil 2:11)

[77]   So far we've done two main things in this document.
First, we've outlined the place of catechesis
    in the Church's mission of evangelization.
Second, we've discussed its relationship
    with various elements of evangelization
    and with other forms of the ministry
        of the word.
Now we want to go on to do several other things.
First, we'll discuss how catechesis is a ministry
    of the whole Church.
Second, we'll describe the fundamental object
    of the catechetical ministry.
Third, we'll list the tasks whereby this object is achieved.
And finally, we'll show how catechesis unfolds gradually
    and has the catechumenate as its inspiration.

Four key dimensions of catechesis

[78]   Catechesis is the work of the Church;
    it's truly an ecclesial act!
The Church is, thus, the *agent* of all catechesis.
In this, animated by the Spirit,
    the Church continues the work of Jesus the Master.
Imitating Mary, the Church proclaims the gospel,
    celebrates it, lives it, and transmits it
    to all who have decided to follow Christ.
The Church transmits the faith
    which the people of the Church also live.
This people of God, who are the Church,
    have an understanding of the mystery of God,
    a vision of the high vocation of being human,
    and a style of life which is joyful,

hopeful,
and loving.
This people who are the Church
transmit the faith actively.
The Church passes on the faith in the hearts
of all those catechumens who come to us,
and they give it back enriched
and profoundly rooted in their own cultures.
The catechumenate, therefore,
is a center of deepening catholicity
and the engine of constant Church renewal.
[79] In a way, the Church is the mother of all who come to her,
the people of God giving birth to children of faith,
nourishing them with catechesis.
The deepest longings of the human heart are thus fed.
[80] If the Church, the people of God, is the *agent*
of all catechesis, as we've just said,
the *goal* of catechesis is to put people in touch,
in communion,
indeed, in intimacy,
with Jesus Christ.
That initial conversion is to the Lord
and to no one or no other thing.
Under the guidance of the Spirit,
that first conversion is strengthened and matured
through catechesis, whereby the new convert
comes to know Christ,
to desire the reign of God,
to understand the requirements,
and to discern his or her path to holiness.
[81] United to Christ this way,
the disciple also unites himself or herself
to everything Christ desires:
unity with the Creator and the Spirit,
unity with the Church,
and unity with all humankind.
[82] If the whole Church is the *agent,*
and the *goal* is intimacy with Christ,

then the *object* of catechesis
is to lead people to profess their faith in Christ.
In baptism this profession is inherently Trinitarian;
we baptize in the name of the Father,
and of the Son,
and of the Holy Spirit.
All catechesis ultimately leads to and matures this moment
in one's life.
Note that this isn't merely a profession of faith
in Jesus as Lord,
though that is surely part of it.
It's more. It's an explicit profession of faith in one God,
Father, Son, and Spirit.
In making this profession of faith,
the Christian is freed from the idolatry
of any human absolute—
be it power, pleasure, race, ancestors,
one's state in life, one's wealth, whatever...
In professing one's faith one shows
that love of God and neighbor
now informs one's life and actions
—not these other forces.
[83] But one cannot profess this faith alone.
It is always in the context of the Church
that the believer steps forward to say
I believe...
In the Church, "I believe" becomes "we believe"
as all the faithful step forward together.
We are fused together
and sometimes this may lead to rejection
by the dominant culture around us.
The martyrs, after all, were witnesses to the faith,
par excellence.
[84] Once again, to review,
the *agent* of catechesis is the whole Church,
its *goal* is intimacy with Christ,
and its *object* is ultimately a profession of faith.

Let us now turn to consider the *tasks* of catechesis
	which are the engine that produce the object.
In understanding the tasks of catechesis,
	we turn, of course, to Christ.
He revealed to his disciples the secrets of the reign of God;
	he taught them to pray;
	he apprenticed them in gospel attitudes;
	he prepared them for mission in his name.
So, too, for us.
	Faith demands, by its very nature,
		to be known,
			celebrated,
			lived,
			and translated into prayer.
But it also demands to be carried forth in mission.
Perhaps Vatican II said it best in its *Declaration on Education*,
	where it is written in article four:
		"catechetical instruction,
		which illumines and strengthens the faith,
		develops a life in harmony with the Spirit of Christ,
		stimulates a conscious and fervent participation
			in the liturgical mystery,
		and encourages men and women to take an active part
			in the apostolate."

Fundamental tasks of catechesis

[85] *Promoting knowledge of the faith*
On the human order,
	when one loves another person,
	he or she desires to know that person
		more and more deeply and profoundly.
So with Christ,
	when one has truly established intimacy with him,
	he or she will desire to know Christ
		ever more deeply.
Catechesis promotes this knowing.

Liturgical education
In the Vatican II document on the liturgy,
	the bishops called the rest of the Church

and themselves
to a more full, active, and conscious participation
in the liturgy of the Church.
Christ, they pointed out in article seven of that document,
is always present in the Church,
especially in the liturgy.
Catechesis promotes a deeper knowledge of the liturgy
and leads to a true "liturgical life" for the disciple.

Moral formation
Conversion to Christ leads inevitably
to walking in his footsteps.
It leads to a profoundly moral life,
based on the teachings of the Master
found in the gospels
and lived in the Church for centuries.
Catechesis promotes knowledge of the Sermon on the Mount
where the Beatitudes are found in Matthew
or the Sermon on the Plain in Luke.
It promotes Christ's understanding
of the "ten commandments" of the Old Covenant.
It promotes, in short, a journey of inner transformation
rooted in the dying and rising
of the Paschal Mystery of Christ himself.

Teaching to pray
Communion with Christ leads to prayer with Christ.
The sentiments with which Jesus prayed
must be ours: adoration, praise, thanksgiving,
trust, supplication, and awe.
All of these are reflected and summed up
in the very prayer which Jesus taught us,
the Lord's Prayer.
Catechesis must teach this prayer with passion
along with other forms of prayer.
It must promote a climate of prayer in the lives
of those to be catechized.
This climate is especially needed

when the gospel's demands are toughest,
or when one feels weak,
or when the mysterious action of God
is discovered in one's life.

Other fundamental tasks of catechesis

[86] *Educating for Community Life*
Community life does not arise spontaneously
but is built up through catechesis
and apprenticeship.
The attitude of Christ, found in Matthew's gospel
must be promoted by catechesis:
simplicity and humility,
solicitude for the least among us,
care for those who are most alienated,
loving and devoted correction,
common prayer,
mutual forgiveness,
and, above all, charity and love in all things.
In developing this community sense,
catechesis must encourage loving attitudes
toward other Christian Churches
and Church communities.
We have much in common with others
and what we share is basic faith:
Sacred Scripture,
grace,
life in Christ based on faith, hope, and charity,
and the interior gifts of the Holy Spirit.
While our own doctrine must be taught clearly,
a suitable knowledge of other churches
can also lead to a more profound faith experience
and give rise to a desire for true unity.
Missionary initiation
Catechesis does not teach the faith
as an end in itself
but leads the disciple to a sense of mission.
This Christian mission
is lived in everyday life at work,

school,
home,
or in cultural and social settings.
It also leads some to a vocation
to priesthood,
to religious life,
to ecclesial lay ministry,
and to missionary work of various kinds.
In this, catechesis promotes what Jesus did:
to seek out the lost sheep,
to proclaim and heal,
to be poor,
to accept rejection and persecution,
to place one's trust firmly in God,
to expect the support of the Spirit,
and to expect no reward
other than the joy of working
for the reign of God.
Here as well there is an ecumenical dimension.
Catechesis prepares believers
to dialogue with people of other faiths.
In this dialogue we will find
our common human origin and end
as well as the seeds of the word
which God has sown in these other faiths.
While such dialogue is important,
announcing the good news is still essential.

Observations about the tasks we've just listed

[87] First, all of these tasks are necessary
for the full growth of the Christian life
just as all the organs are needed
in the human body.
Second, each task, in its own way,
also achieves the goal of catechesis.
Hence, moral formation occurs in the Church
but leads to social values.
Yet, third, these tasks are interdependent,
one naturally leading to the other

—and back again.
>Hence, knowing one's faith leads to mission
>>and sacramental life leads to moral transformation.
Fourth, two principal means are used to accomplish these tasks:
>passing on the gospel
>and experiencing the Christian life.
>>Hence, moral formation inevitably leads
>>>to a lived reality
>>>and liturgical formation to life in Christ.
Fifth, each task is both a gift of the Spirit
>and a demand of the Christian life.
>>Hence, while faith is a gift, for example,
>>>there is a duty to study and grow in it.
Sixth, each dimension of the faith, like faith itself,
>must be rooted in human experience
>and not merely remain on the outskirts of life.
>>Hence, knowing one's faith enlightens all life,
>>>common prayer becomes profoundly personal,
>>>morality is rooted in deep human values,
>>>and prayer opens to all social problems.

The baptismal catechumenate

[88] The four stages of the baptismal catechumenate
>should be reflected in all proper catechesis:

The pre-catechumenate
This is the early and initial turning of one's life
>to Christ
>and the truths of the gospel.

The catechumenate
The place where catechesis occurs
>in the handing on of the gospels.

The time of purification and illumination
The more intense period of preparation
>for the sacraments of initiation
>where the Creed and the Lord's Prayer
>>take center stage.

The period of mystagogy
The experience of the sacraments themselves
>and entry into community life.

[89] These are the ancient steps by which catechesis
has served the Church
since the earliest years of our history.
If catechetical ministry in today's Church
is, indeed, linked to conversion and a decision for Christ,
it will follow this model
and provide both a gradual and Christ-centered
experience of faith.
[90] It must be noted, however, that most of those
who are receiving catechesis today
are already baptized and are not catechumens.
They have, therefore, the grace of baptism
and are already introduced into the Church
as children of God.
[91] Nonetheless, there are some elements
of the baptismal catechumenate
that are a source of inspiration
for post-baptismal catechesis.
First, we are reminded by the baptismal catechumenate
of the importance of initiation
into the Christian life through baptism/confirmation,
and Eucharist.
Second, the baptismal catechumenate is the duty
of the entire Christian community, especially the sponsors.
Likewise post-baptismal catechesis:
the entire parish is responsible for it,
and it should not be left only to pastors and catechists.
Third, the baptismal catechumenate
is closely linked to the Paschal Mystery
and the Easter Vigil's celebration of baptism.
Likewise all catechesis should be inspired
by this spirituality.
Fourth, the baptismal catechumenate receives people
in all their cultural situations and ties.
Likewise all catechetical activity brings into the Church
authentic "seeds of the word"
planted by God through people and nations.

Fifth, the baptismal catechumenate
> is a *process of formation and a school of faith.*
>> Likewise post-baptismal catechesis should occur
>> in stages, unfolding gradually throughout life.

In short, even though post-baptismal catechesis is not identical
> with the baptismal catechumenate,
>> it does well to draw on and be enriched by these elements of it.

The Gospel Message

"This is eternal life, that they may know you, the only true God,
and Jesus Christ whom you have sent." (Jn 17:3)

Introduction to part two

[92]   The Christian faith has two aspects.
First, it is believing the word of God
and committing oneself to it.
And second, it is trying to understand better
the mystery of the word.
[93]   This chapter will deal with the latter
and it will have two parts.
The first chapter of part two
sets out the norms and criteria which catechesis must follow
in order to accomplish its task.
The second chapter examines the content of the faith
as presented in the *Catechism of the Catholic Church*
which is the doctrinal point of reference
for all catechesis.
This chapter also sets out some criteria
by which local Churches might prepare
their own catechisms based on this one,
to serve diverse circumstances and cultures.

Chapter One

Norms and criteria for presenting the gospel message in catechesis

"And the Word became flesh and lived among us." (Jn 1:14)

[94] The source from which catechesis draws its message
is, of course, the word of God.
This word is entrusted to the Church,
which is the people of God,
and the people know that this word
is Jesus Christ himself.
Because of the incarnation this divine word,
without ceasing to be divine,
is also expressed now in human words.
Yet it remains a mystery requiring interpretation,
reflection,
and care.
The Church does this;
we who are the Church listen to the word devotedly,
we guard it with dedication,
and we expound it faithfully.
[95] Hence, the word of God,
recorded in both Scripture and Tradition,
is understood more deeply by means
of the sense of faith of all the people of God,
guided by the Magisterium.
It is celebrated in liturgy
where it is proclaimed, heard, interiorized, and explained.
It shines forth in the lives of faithful people
who have lived in the Church down through the ages.
It is deepened by theological research.
And it is unmistakably visible in the world
as people live their religious and moral values
which, as "seeds of the word,"
are sown in human society and diverse cultures.

[96] The three primary sources of catechesis
            are closely related to each other.
Sacred Scripture, first of all, is God's own speech
            put down under the influence of the Spirit.
Sacred Tradition, secondly, transmits this divine speech
            down through history to us today.
And the Magisterium gives it an authentic interpretation.
These three primary sources
            provide a variety of "documents of faith"
                    biblical excerpts,
                    liturgical texts,
                    patristic writings,
                    formulations of the Magisterium,
                    creeds,
                    testimonies of the saints,
                    and theological reflections.
Taken together these documents of faith,
            all deriving from the word of God,
            provide catechists with five important *standards*
                    by which to evaluate their work.
We're going to spend considerable time now
            reflecting on how these five standards are applied
                    to the work of catechesis in the Church.

[97] Here, first, is a list of those five standards.
One, the message passed on through catechesis
            centers on the person of Jesus Christ,
            leading naturally to the Trinity.
Two, the Good News proclaimed in catechesis
            centers on the gift of salvation
            which is a message of liberation.
Three, catechesis occurs within the Church
            leading to an understanding
            of its continuity through history.
Four, the Good News is destined for peoples
            of all cultures in the world
            and is, therefore, expressed and lived in various ways.
Five, the gospel message treats divine revelation completely

and orders itself in such a way
that men and women can come to understand it.

Jesus is the Center leading to the Trinity

[98] Jesus Christ not only transmits God's word;
Jesus *is* that word
and all catechesis is completely tied to him.
What does this mean?
First, what we find at the heart of all catechesis
is not a book or a theology system,
but a person!
The fundamental task of catechesis is to present Christ
and everything in relation to him,
leading people to follow Christ in their lives.
Second, Christ is the event toward which
all salvation history converges.
Catechesis helps people see themselves
in relation to that.
Third, none of what catechists teach
comes from themselves.
Catechists pass on the unchanged teaching of Jesus.
The gospels have an inherently catechetical structure,
expressing the teachings first proposed
in the early Church
and passed down through history to us.
[99] Fourth, the reality of Jesus Christ leads to the Trinity.
We confess Jesus, Son of the Father, in the power of the Spirit.
[100] Catechesis is molded in this formula:
"through Christ to the Father in the Holy Spirit."
Catechesis shows the intimate life of the Trinity,
starting with God's works of salvation.
Catechesis leads people to see themselves in light of God,
bound together in community,
and equal in personal dignity.

Salvation and liberation

[101] First we will consider salvation.
The message of Jesus about God
is good news for all human beings.

It is an amazing announcement that, in Christ,
    we are saved and set free!
This great gift of God liberates us
    from oppression,
    from sin,
    and from the power of darkness.
As catechesis transmits this message
    it is gradually deepened and developed.
[102] Here are some key notions related to this:
First, God is not distant or inaccessible;
    God is present among us all
    and God's power is divine love.
        In short, we can say simply,
        "God is our Father."
Second, Jesus shows us that God offers us salvation
    (the liberation we shall discuss in a moment),
    and makes us sons and daughters of God.
        This begins now in this life
        but it is fully achieved in eternity.
Third, the reign of God announced by Jesus
    is one of justice, love, and peace.
        Simply put, "God is just."
        This is Good News for those denied justice,
          and for those who struggle
          to reinstate it.
Fourth, this reign of God is brought into existence
    in Jesus' very person.
Fifth, the Church is at the service of the reign of God,
    in which God hopes to shelter all peoples.
Finally, Jesus shows us that the human race
    is not journeying toward nothingness
    but is, in fact, in pilgrimage to God's house.
[103] Now we will turn to liberation.
Jesus addressed the poor in his preaching,
      assuring them that, even though they suffer now,
      they would inherit and enter the reign of God.
In the Beatitudes, Jesus made plain that, in the long run,
    the kingdom of God
    is not concurrent with any kingdoms on Earth.

The Church today shares Jesus' care for the poor,
       rejected,
       illiterate,
       hungry,
       and ill-treated.
The gospel promises these people liberation,
       which is a radical freedom,
       and the Church must help bring justice into reality now.
[104] Toward this end, catechesis is attentive to the following.
First, the liberation of which we speak here
       embraces the total person
       and is also religious.
It is not confined to any single sphere of human experience,
       such as the economic, political, social, or doctrinal.
              It is, indeed, all of these and more:
              it leads to the Absolute, which is God.
Second, our understanding of social morality
       is that Christ is *the* Liberator,
       historically and presently.
              In this the great commandment to love
              is fulfilled.
Third, catechesis should arouse in the learner
       a "preferential option for the poor,"
       which implies a commitment to justice
              according to each one's situation in life.

Catechesis occurs within the Church

[105] Faith lives in the hearts of all believers,
       who are the Church.
Hence, when faith is "passed on" from one to another,
       it is the Church's faith of which we speak.
The Christian community has received the gospel
       and the community is responsible
              to understand it,
              celebrate it,
              live it,
              and communicate it to the world.
This faith has been held and lived
       down through the centuries by

42

apostles,

martyrs,

saints,

doctors of the Church,

missionaries,

theologians,

pastors,

and all those who believe.

[106] Although spread throughout the world
in many different cultures,
we Christians hold *one* faith.

There is, as Scripture says in Ephesians, chapter 4,
"one Lord, one Faith, one baptism,
one God and Father of us all."

Catechesis nourishes this unity.

[107] The Church exists in time.

This means that we have a long history and memory
of the saving events of the past,
and we make them known through catechesis.

This also means that we interpret present events
in light of the gospel
to see how God's Spirit is today renewing the face of the earth.

This also means that we believe in a future,
we expect the consummation of the kingdom of God
to occur.

[108] Catechesis, therefore, must pay attention to the following.

First, catechesis should present salvation history
by means of biblical catechesis,
beginning with the Old Testament
and culminating in Christ.

We should also teach the history of the Church
which is the story of the people of God.

Second, catechesis should examine the "signs of the times"
and illuminate them in light of our history.

Third, catechesis should situate the sacraments
within salvation history
by means of reflection on the mysteries we celebrate
with an eye to their historical link
as the avenue to salvation for humans.

Fourth, catechesis should look "behind" the events,
   both historical events and present ones
   to find the mystery of God in them.
   There we will find God's plan for salvation.

The Good News is destined for peoples of all cultures

[109] Jesus Christ lived in a specific time and place;
   he lived in a first-century culture.
This reality is the first "inculturation" of God's word.
   It is also the model for the way we organize
      evangelization today.
In a gradual and global process,
   the gospel is penetrating the deepest levels
   of people and cultures,
      transforming them in faith.
Governed by two basic criteria,
   the Christian community decides
   which dimensions of each culture are fitting
      and which are not.
The criteria are (1) compatibility with the gospel
   and (2) communion with the universal Church.
All of the people of God must be involved in this process.
[110] Here are some concrete ways this is realized.
First, the community itself is the principal agent,
   working through catechists
   who are rooted in their own cultures.
Second, local catechisms are a good tool toward this end.
Third, the baptismal catechumenate
   and catechetical programs
   should be "centers of inculturation."
      They can bring local language,
         symbols,
         and values into play.
Fourth, catechesis can help people become articulate
   in their faith
   and, thus, speak clearly about Christian hope
      in unconverted or post-christian cultures.
[111] In its task of inculturating the gospel,
   catechesis must present its message

with integrity and purity,
    just as Jesus did.
Those coming to faith have a right to receive the gospel
    in all its rigor and vigor,
    not mutilated, falsified, or diminished.
[112] There are two closely connected dimensions to this.
First, God revealed the divine wonders to us humans
    progressively and gradually,
    and catechesis should do the same in its work.
In this way, the entire gospel message will be preached,
    adapted to the capacity of those being catechized,
        and gradually proposed more amply
        until the full gospel message is announced.
Second, the demands of the gospel should not be reduced
    for fear of its rejection.
It must be presented with authenticity,
    even when translated into various cultural settings.
It must, therefore, take into account the people
    to whom it is addressed,
    but care should be taken to safeguard its authenticity
        when transposing it.
[113] In short, inculturation occurs successfully
    when the entire gospel is preached
    in a culturally sensitive way
        without falling either into closed inflexibility
        or facile accommodation,
            either of which enfeebles the gospel
            and secularizes the Church.

A complete message, ordered for good understanding

[114] We have already said here
    that the gospel message should be presented
    in its entirety, leaving nothing out.
This leads us to say as well
    that certain truths illumine others
    and should be presented early in the catechetical process
        while others follow on those fundamental points
        and can be presented later in the process.

[115] Here is a list of the most central points.
First, the history of God's words and actions
    on behalf of us humans
    as it unfolds in the Old Testament
        and culminates in the New.
Second, the Apostles Creed
    which is a vital synthesis of the faith
    and the key to all the Church's doctrine.
Third, the sacraments which regenerate us constantly
    and spring from the Paschal Mystery itself.
        The Eucharist is center point of the Christian life
            and the other sacraments are related to it.
Fourth, the commandment to love God and neighbor,
        lived in the spirit of the Beatitudes,
        and constituting the *magna carta* of the Christian life.
Fifth, the Lord's own Prayer,
        gathering as it does the essence of the gospel,
        making clear the childlike trust with which
            we can turn to God.
[116] This is a very important point:
catechesis presents the gospel of Jesus Christ
        to human beings
        who find within it the very meaning of life itself.
The gospel illumines, if you will,
        the whole of life.
In other words, in the incarnation,
        God revealed God's own self, yes,
        but God also revealed us to ourselves
            in the person of Jesus Christ.
In the light of the gospel, then,
        we see ourselves as we truly are:
            sons and daughters of God
            fully able to love and live moral lives.
The very purpose of catechesis
        is to help the human person
            live in communion with Jesus Christ.
[117] Therefore, human experience is vital in catechesis.
It is, in a sense, the starting point

since it contains within it the "clues of God"
        which the believer uses to discover Faith.
Five points follow from this.
First, all pre-catechesis shows how the gospel
        fully satisfies the longing of the human heart.
Second, catechesis helps interpret human life
        in light of the experiences of the people of Israel,
                of Jesus Christ,
                and of the Church,
                in which the Spirit of the risen Christ lives today.
Third, catechesis shows how the themes of the Creed:
        creation,
        sin,
        incarnation,
        Easter,
        Pentecost,
        and the endtimes
                can illuminate human life.
Fourth, human virtues, planted within us by God,
        are raised up and promoted
        by catechesis on the Beatitudes,
                leading to a moral life.
Fifth, great human experiences such as
        birth and death,
        welcoming,
        meal times,
        reconciliation,
        healing,
        marriage,
        and ministry,
                are the reference for liturgical catechesis
                and are deeply rooted in culture.
[118] It isn't possible to say beforehand
        in what order the central points of the Faith
        should be presented in catechesis.
It is possible, for example, to begin with God
        in order to arrive at Christ,
        or vice versa.

47

It is possible to start with human life
      in order to come around to God,
      and conversely.
The order in which the main points are presented
      must be conditioned by circumstances
      and by the level of faith of those to be catechized.
Local bishops should draw up norms
      to help with this.

Chapter Two

"This is our faith, this is the faith of the Church"

"So then, brothers and sisters, stand firm and hold fast to the tradition that you were taught by us." (2 Thes 2:15)

[119] The Church has always used short documents
    to state the faith:
        New Testament texts,
        creeds,
        and liturgical prayers.
In recent years, the Church has used catechisms
    which are official Church documents
    and which give a comprehensive treatment of faith.
        Catechisms can be universal or local.
        (The *Catechism of the Catholic Church* is universal.)
We're going to take some time now
    to comment on both kinds of catechisms.
[120] But first this note:
    The *Catechism of the Catholic Church* (CCC)
        which we're going to discuss now,
    and the *General Directory for Catechesis* (GDC)
        which you're reading,
            are complementary.
The CCC is a statement of the Church's faith
    and of Catholic doctrine
    rising from Sacred Scripture,
        the Apostolic Tradition,
        and the Church's Magisterium
            (or official teaching office).
The GDC is a tool to help us teach well what's in the CCC.
    It's also an official document,
    drawing both from the Magisterium and Vatican II.

The Catechism of the Catholic Church

[121] The purpose of the CCC,
    as stated in its own prologue,

is to present the essential and fundamental
  contents of Catholic doctrine on both faith and morals
    in a systematic way
    and in light of Vatican II
    and the whole of the Church's Tradition.
It desires to promote unity within the Church
  by helping us hold to one faith.
It is an obligatory point of reference for all catechesis
  and assures those to be catechized
  that they will receive the full and official message of faith.
It is not intended to replace local catechisms
  but to serve as the source for them.
Unlike other documents of the Church's Magisterium,
  this one is a full synthesis of the Faith
  with a universal function.
[122] The CCC is structured around four dimensions of faith:
  the profession of faith,
  the celebration of the liturgy,
  the morality of the gospel,
  and prayer.
This structure reflects the essential aspects of faith itself:
  to believe in the Triune God and salvation,
  to be made holy by God in sacramental life,
  to love God with all one's heart and one's neighbor as oneself,
  and to pray with hope, expecting the coming of the reign of God.
This structure also reflects the pillars of catechesis:
  the Creed,
  the sacraments,
  the Ten Commandments,
  the Lord's Prayer.
It should be noted that the best structure for catechesis itself
  cannot be mandated by a universal catechism
  because it must be culturally sensitive to be effective.
    The CCC provides only a doctrinal point of reference,
    not a way of teaching these things effectively.
Perfect fidelity to Catholic doctrine is fully compatible
  with a rich diversity in presentation.
[123] The CCC is oriented around two poles.

First, the mystery of the Triune God
and how God touches us humans
runs through the entire work.
Second, the mystery of the human person
created, saved, and sustained by God,
also runs through the entire work.
The doctrine of the CCC can, indeed,
be distilled into this remark
found in Vatican II's *Constitution on the Church in Today's World*:
"Christ the new Adam,
in the very revelation of the mystery of the Father
and of his love,
fully reveals humanity to itself
and brings to light its very high calling"
(article 22).
[124] The CCC is a catechism.
This means it is an official text of the Church,
that it is precise,
and that it is at the same time complete.
It does not present as doctrine
private opinions or views held by certain schools
and not by others.
It is, moreover, universal
and incorporates the doctrine of Vatican II
as well as religious and moral concerns of our times.
However, it does *not* mean to provide
catechetical methods for local communities
which must be fashioned according to
culture,
age,
spiritual maturity,
and social conditions.
The latter needs are addressed by local catechisms,
and mainly by catechists themselves.
[125] Vatican II desired to *conserve* "the deposit of faith"
given to the Church by Christ himself,
and also to *present it* more adequately for modern times.
The CCC has that same goal.

The CCC rises out of Tradition and Scripture.
By using it as a reference, one can be assured
that he or she will pass on the faith
in its entirely.
[126] We will now examine the relationship of the CCC
first, with Sacred Scripture,
and then with the tradition of ancient Church writers.
[127] In any ministry of the word,
(of which catechesis is one part)
Sacred Scripture has a preeminent position.
Catechesis must be filled to the marrow
with the spirit of the gospel
understood in the context of the Church itself.
The CCC provides this Church understanding.
[128] The CCC and Sacred Scripture, then,
are both sources of inspiration for catechesis
and each in its own way functions
to nourish and inform catechetical work.
The content of God's word must be made plain by catechesis,
and both the texts of Scripture
and those of the CCC are the vehicles of this task.
Catechumens should have access to both Scripture
and the local catechism
which are the "documents of faith" being handed on.
[129] Now, turning to ancient Church writers,
their sayings are a sure witness
to the presence of Tradition in the Church.
They bring pastoral and doctrinal richness to the Church.
We pay special attention to the following.
First, they give decisive importance
to the baptismal catechumenate
in the structure of the Church.
Second, they witness to the gradual, progressive nature
of Christian formation where, like the people of Israel,
they speak of the journey to baptism
as an unfolding process in one's life.
Third, the catechesis of the ancient writers
begins with the narration of salvation history,

moves to the Creed and the Lord's Prayer during Lent,
and then to a period of reflection on the mysteries
after the Easter celebration.
[130] The CCC brings a certain truth dimension
and reminds us how necessary it is to have
a knowledge of one's faith, however simple in form.
It also provides for an education in faith,
rooted in all its sources.
All in all, the CCC results in a sevenfold approach:
the three phases in speaking of salvation history:
the Old Testament,
the life of Jesus,
the history of the Church,
and the four pillars in teaching about this:
the Creed,
the sacraments,
the Ten Commandments,
and the Lord's Prayer.
Various ways of teaching this should be developed
for local situations.

Catechisms in the local Churches
[131] The CCC is meant to encourage and assist
in the writing of new local catechisms.
These local catechisms vary in their cultural situations
while carefully preserving the unity of faith
and Catholic doctrine.
Pope John Paul II has called for this
in an Apostolic Exhortation in 1979
dealing with catechetics.
Such local catechisms, he said,
must be prepared or approved by local bishops,
in concert with the Holy See,
and up-to-date in method.
[132] Here are the three characteristics to be found
in every local catechism.
First, they are to be treated as "official" documents,
and, as such, are formally part of the Tradition
of the Church.

In this way, they differ from other catechetical tools
    such as all unofficial catechisms, guides, or other texts.
Second, local catechisms, like all catechisms,
    present the fundamental truths of the Christian mystery
    in a systematic and complete manner,
        honoring the idea that some truths
            are more central than others,
    but also in the richness of local languages
    and cultural settings.
Third, the local catechism, alongside the Sacred Scriptures,
    is a point of reference for catechists.
But while these texts are both important,
    they aren't all there is:
        the person of the catechist,
        the method of teaching,
        the rapport between catechist and disciple,
        respect for the learning capability of the disciple,
        an atmosphere of love and faith,
        the involvement of the entire community.
            All these are also very important
            alongside the local catechism and the Scriptures.
[133] Every local catechism must assemble all aspects
    of the faith in a systematic way.
But they must also adapt this presentation
    to the culture,
        age,
        spiritual maturity,
        and social conditions of the local Church.
Vatican II said that such adaptations "must ever be the law
    of all evangelization" (*Church in Today's World*, article 44).
So first, local catechisms do not merely repeat
    the language of the CCC
    but do, indeed, present the faith
        with reference to the local culture.
Second, local catechisms must refer to the experiences
    in the lives of the local people
    and be close to the mentality of those for whom it is intended.

Third, they should pay attention to the way
        the Church is experienced in the culture
        for which they are intended.
        There's a difference between a society
        where religious indifference dominates
                and one that is profoundly religious.
Fourth, they should take into account
        problems arising from local social conditions,
        especially economics, politics, and family customs.
                They should present Catholic social teaching
                        in a way that assists local people
                        to do critical theological reflection.
And finally, as we said in part one, chapter one of this document,
        the situation of the local Church
        should also be addressed by the local catechism.
[134] Local Churches must be creative and guided by the Spirit
        in designing their catechisms.
In this way, they will both present the faith well
        and also be effective.
[135] We wish to emphasize the following in this regard:
First, a mere summary of the CCC
        is not the same as a true local catechism,
        and it is the latter we most want.
Second, local catechisms can be diocesan,
        regional,
        or national in character.
Third, the CCC does not dictate the structure
        of the local catechism.
        Indeed, some will be structured along biblical lines,
                others along trinitarian ones,
                others according to stages of salvation,
                others following the liturgical year.
Fourth, while the CCC is a secure reference text,
        local catechisms, without sacrificing essential truths,
        must transpose this message
                into a language which will be understood
                by the people who will use it.
As Pope John XXIII said in his opening speech at Vatican II,

and the document on the *Church in Today's World* echoes,
　　"The deposit of faith is one thing,
　　the manner of expressing it is quite another."
[136] The CCC and local catechisms
　　together express a "symphony of the faith"
　　when they are in harmony.
Such a universal chorus has a deep theological meaning:
　　It manifests true catholicity in one Church.
　　It expresses the communion of local Churches in one faith.
　　It expresses the reality of episcopal collegiality.

Part Three

The Art of Teaching the Faith

*"And when Jesus was alone, those who were about him with the twelve
asked him concerning the parable. And he said to them, 'to you has been
given the secret of the kingdom of God.'"* (Mk 4:10–11, 34)

[137] Jesus Christ is the first catechist.
    He was not only teacher but also friend to his disciples.
    He lived what he preached.
    He asked opportune questions and explained
        to his disciples what he taught the crowds.
    He introduced them to prayer.
    He sent them as missionaries and sent his Spirit with them.
        Indeed, this is the "teaching style of God,"
        the model for all we do.
[138] We are now going to examine this more deeply:
    first, how the Spirit works through catechists,
    and second, how this translates into catechetical activity.

Chapter One

*The teaching style of God,
source and model
for the art of teaching the faith*

[139] To truly help a person encounter God,
which is the task of the catechist,
means to emphasize
the relationship that the person has with God
so that he or she can be guided by God.
God will then transform the events in the life of this person
into lessons of wisdom and liberation,
and the person will grow progressively toward maturity.
[140] Jesus is the perfection of this divine teaching style.
In Christ, the disciples learned how to pass on the faith:
calling the poor and rejected to them,
proclaiming the reign of God,
living a delicate but strong love
which liberated them from evil
and promoted a common life,
taking on a lifestyle which reflects this teaching:
hope in the Kingdom
and charity to one's neighbor.
using all Christ's methods:
word, silence, metaphor,
image, example, and signs.
[141] And now the Church,
a sacrament of Christ to the world,
is a *living catechesis* when the people of God
proclaim,
celebrate,
and live in the reign of God.
Down through the centuries,
in a variety of forms
(catechumenate, catechisms, religious life, and others)
the Church has continued God's teaching style
in Christ under the power of the Holy Spirit.
[142] There cannot be teachers of the faith

other than those who are convinced and faithful
followers of Christ and the Church.
[143] For its part, the ministry of catechesis
is always, therefore, inspired by faith itself
and by Christ's own teaching style.
Under the guidance of the Spirit
it leads people to a true experience of faith.
It underlines the divine initiative,
loving motivation, and respect of our freedom
on God's part.
It highlights the dignity of the gift of faith
and the demand to grow in faith
on our part.
It follows the principle that faith unfolds slowly
and is adapted to different cultures.
It keeps Jesus the center of all faith
and the gospel the center of life.
It values community
which is proper to the people of God
who are the Church.
It is rooted in interpersonal relationships
where God is in dialogue with the believer.
It links words and deeds,
teaching and experience.
And, finally, it draws its power from the love of God,
and takes the form of a process or a journey
leading to mature faith.

[144] God's wonderful dialogue with every human being
is the inspiration for catechesis.
Hence it is neither of a purely divine form,
without human interests,
nor merely of human form
without the divine presence.
It takes the form of God's own dialogue,
echoing it tirelessly,
and it seeks several objects.
First, to promote a growing sense of the connection

between our assent in faith
and the content of the Christian message.
Second, to develop all the dimensions of faith:
knowing, celebrating, living, and praying.
Third, to move the person to abandon him or herself
completely and freely to God:
intelligence, will, heart, and memory.
And fourth, to help one discern one's vocation.

[145] Genuine catechesis helps discern the action of God
in the life of the believer
through a climate of listening, thanksgiving, and prayer.
It likewise encourages active participation
among those to be catechized.
[146] God speaks to us in ways we can understand.
Likewise catechesis must seek a language
that effectively communicates the word of God.
Only by God's grace can this be done.
The Holy Spirit gives us the joy of doing it.
Therefore, catechesis permits the communication
of the whole word of God
in the concrete everyday lives of people.
[147] Toward this end, the catechist must know and use
those educational tools and methods
that can be applied in this ministry.

Chapter Two

[148] The Church assumes those methods for teaching
    that can rightly be placed at the service
      of the gospel.
There are a variety of methods, therefore,
    not just one.
[149] There is a connection between method and content,
    with method at the service of content.
The nature of the message determines, in part,
    how it will be taught.
So, for example, a biblical method might work well.
    The telling of the stories of faith might, too.
    The use of liturgical signs is effective.
    Using mass media also has its place.

The method of teaching
[150-151] We must always remember
    that the communication of faith
    is an event of grace.
        Simply put, God is acting in people's lives.
With this in mind, catechesis seeks the most effective way
    to make this understood,
    to make it plain.
We speak of two methods of presentation:
    the inductive
    and the deductive.
The inductive begins with such things as
    biblical events,
    liturgical acts,
    events in the Church's life
    or events in daily life
        so as to discern the meaning they might have
            in divine Revelation.
This method has many advantages

because it matches the way God has chosen
to reveal the divine mystery to us.
It also connects to a profound human urge
to know the mysterious
through visible signs.
This approach is also sometimes called
"existential" or "ascending"
because it begins with experiences
and enlightens them with the word of God.
The deductive method, on the other hand,
explains and describes doctrine and principles first.
One then comes to understand experience
by deriving conclusions from such principles.
This approach is also sometimes called
"kerygmatic" or "descending"
because it begins with Scripture, doctrine, or liturgy
and applies them to life.
Both methods are legitimate and needed.

The role of human experience
[152-153] Human experience is the stuff of life.
Its place in catechesis must be continuously evaluated.
First, it arouses interest,
questions,
hopes and fears,
and reflections and judgments in us.
Catechesis has the task of making people more aware
of their most basic human experiences
so they become aware of God's hand in their lives.
Second, human experience points to the divine
because there is an inborn hunger for union with God.
Reflecting on experience is therefore necessary
if the truths of Revelation are to be understood at all.
Third, experience is, in fact, the very place in human life
where salvation occurs.
The catechist must teach the person
to read his or her own lived experience
so as to see in it
God reaching us with grace and saving us.

In this regard, the great questions of life
are most able to lead one to the divine heart:
        the existence of God,
        the destiny of the human person,
        the origin and end of history,
        the truth about good and evil,
        the meaning of suffering,
                of love,
                and of the future.
Interpreting and illuminating human experience
        through the eyes of faith, even when difficult,
                is how the revealed message and human experiences
                connect and lead one to faith.
This has been true in the proclamation of the prophets,
        the preaching of Christ himself,
        the teaching of the apostles,
        and the whole history of the Christian Church.

Memorization
[154] It's important that those who are to be catechized
        memorize certain prayers and lists
        which are part of the legacy of the Christian faith.
Such memorization should not be mechanical
        and should only be encouraged
        after sufficient catechesis has occurred,
                so that it is understood fully
                and appreciated deeply,
                creating a *desire to remember.*
Memorization takes its place among other methods of teaching,
        including spontaneous reaction,
                quiet reflection,
                dialogue with others,
                occasional silence,
                and written responses.
[155] Again, it's important that the disciple
        be *formed in the faith,*
        and not merely taught facts about faith

even though the facts of the faith are important
in the journey toward mature faith.

The person of the catechist
[156] Nothing—not the method
or the texts,
or any other part of the program—
is more important than *the person of the catechist*
in every phase of the catechetical process.
The gifts given to the catechist by the Spirit
to witness faithfully
and live accordingly
are the very soul of catechetical ministry.
The catechist is a mediator,
facilitating communication
between people and the mystery of God,
among those being catechized,
and between them and the larger community.
Because of this, the catechist is called to a Christian way of life
that reflects his or her beliefs well.
The relationship between the catechist
and those to be catechized
is also critical.

Those to be catechized
[157] Those to be catechized cannot be passive recipients
but must be actively engaged in the process
through prayer,
participation in the sacraments,
the liturgy,
parish life,
social commitments,
works of charity,
and the promotion of human values.
Catechesis, after all, is a process of taking on
a way of life and personal conversion,
not the acquisition of a body of information.

The community's role
[158] It's also important to note
that catechetical activity occurs within a community.
The community teaches by how it lives as a body:
welcoming new people,
encouraging growth in faith,
and connecting people to one another.

Small groups
[159] Catechesis will often occur in small groups,
which are a reflection of the larger community
and in which people connect more closely.

Media
[160] Well-planned catechetical programs
must use all the modern media available to them
in order to be fully effective.
[161] In fact, it's more than merely bringing media
into the classroom setting.
It involves making a serious commitment
to integrating the Christian message
into the new culture of modern media
using new languages,
new techniques,
and a new psychology.
[162] Those who work in the mass media
have a huge role to play in this,
as well as families and the young generations.
The media should help make the gospel present
by animating a passion for the truth,
working in defense of liberty,
respecting the dignity of all,
and elevating the culture of peoples.

Part Four

Those to Be Catechized

"Jesus unrolled the scroll:...'The Spirit of the Lord is upon me, because he has anointed me to bring good news to the poor.'" (Lk 4:16–21)

[163] Jesus made himself a catechist of the kingdom of God,
    announcing a joyful message
    to the ones in society who were most disadvantaged.
But the Good News which Jesus proclaimed
    is for all persons,
    no matter where they live,
    what their backgrounds,
        their social situations,
        their health,
        or their lifestyles.
Jesus is for *all*. Period.
    And now Jesus sends us,
    just as he did his own disciples,
        to teach as he did
        and to announce his reign.
[164] Through its history,
    the Church has continued Jesus' work.
[165] Catechesis must be shaped in such a way
    that it communicates well
    the message of Jesus to those being catechized.
The method of teaching changes in order to address
    different kinds of people.
[166] In this section, we will deal with four aspects of catechesis:
    how to adapt catechesis well,
    how to adjust for age,
    how to adjust for those in special situations,
    and how to adjust for various contexts.

Chapter One

Adaptation to those to be catechized: general aspects

[167] All the baptized are called by God
    to mature faith
    and have a right to sufficient catechesis.
People live in concrete situations in life,
    and catechesis must occur there
        so the recipient is active and conscious
            and not merely a silent spectator.
[168] Of course, it's really the entire community
    which is being catechized all the time,
        making this a genuine community concern.
[169] The model for catechetical adaptation
    is nothing less than the Incarnation itself,
        where God took into account the human situation
            and addressed us where we really live.
Likewise the catechist must address those to be catechized
    in their real life situations, no matter how diverse,
        making the gospel genuine nourishment for life.
[170] The differences which catechetical adaptation
    takes into account include culture,
        age,
        spiritual maturity,
        social and local Church conditions.
But it isn't merely external conditions
    that adaptation addresses;
        it also pays attention to the inner life
            of women and men
            which is where they meet God.

Chapter Two

Catechesis according to age

[171] The Christian life is one
   that requires constant renewal,
   which is the role that catechesis plays.
The various stages in the journey of faith
   must be properly integrated
   into an ongoing catechetical experience
      which begins at faith's inception
      and lasts for a lifetime!
We're going to give here some general principles
   under which catechesis can be adapted
   for various stages of life and faith.

Adult catechesis
[172] When we provide catechesis to adults,
   we must take into account their experience,
      their life journey,
      and the challenges they've encountered.
There are those adults who live their faith
   and desire a deeper experience.
There are also those who, although baptized,
   have been inadequately catechized,
      or are inactive or indifferent.
And then there are non-baptized adults
   with whom the catechumenate is concerned.
And finally, there are adults who come
   from other Christian traditions
   not in full communion with the Catholic Church.
[173] The faith of adults must be continually developed,
   giving a sense of hope in life's situations.
How adult catechesis is done—and who does it—
   is vitally important.
[174] To this end, we must consider
   the diverse conditions of life,
   including problems and challenges,
      in which adults live.

We must consider the universal call to holiness
    which everyone has.
We must consider how the community
    welcomes and supports adults.
And we must integrate liturgical formation
    with catechesis, alongside the service of charity.

[175] Adult catechesis, then,
        must be systematic and comprehensive,
        following the Church's teachings faithfully.
It must proclaim salvation first and foremost,
        pointing out the obstacles to salvation
        which are prevalent today.
And it must lead adults
        to a faith-filled reading of Sacred Scripture
        and to prayer.
Here are its specific tasks.
First, it should promote formation in the life of the risen Christ,
        by suitable means such as
        meaningful celebrations of the sacraments,
            retreats,
            and spiritual direction.
Second, it should lead adults to evaluate social and cultural changes
        in the light of faith,
        discerning true values in these complex times.
Third, it should clarify the religious and moral questions
        of our day and time.
Fourth, it should clarify the relationship
        between the Church's actions
        and the actions of governments and other temporal agencies,
            by building on the Church's social teachings.
Fifth, it should promote the pastoral aim of Christian thought,
        thereby avoiding fundamentalism
        and "private" interpretation of the Church's teachings.
And finally, it should encourage adults
        to take firm hold of the Church's mission
        and to provide a strong Christian witness in society.
Overall, adults in catechesis should be led

to see themselves for what they are,
   living their faith in a real time and place.
      In this way they avoid losing their individual identities
      in a society which tends to standardize people
         and render them anonymous.
[176] There are several forms of adult catechesis
   which we will now list.
But note, all of these are meant only to accompany
   the ongoing, systematic catechetical courses
   which every parish must provide for all adults.
First, of course, is the RCIA,
   where folks are readied for Christian initiation.
Second are the traditional forms of adult catechesis,
   following the liturgical year
   or in the form of parish missions.
Third is the formation of catechists themselves,
   and others in lay ministry.
Fourth is preparation for marriage,
   or for the baptism of one's children,
   as well as for other critical moments in one's life.
Fifth occurs at times of change,
   such as when joining the military
   or when emigrating.
Sixth deals with the use of leisure time
   during holidays or vacations.
Seventh addresses special events in the life of the Church.

Catechesis of infants and young children
[177] Christ proclaimed the children to be
   privileged participants in the reign of God.
Therefore, those who have given life to children
   and baptized them in faith,
   must also provide them with ongoing catechesis.
[178] Various members of a child's circle of life
   play a role in catechesis.
Here are some characteristics of that work.
First, infancy and childhood should be seen
   as an important time in the development of faith

especially as they prepare a child
   to grow in faith later.
Second, it is traditional that initiation is completed
   during this period of life,
   culminating in reception of the Eucharist.
Third, central in this is formation in prayer
   and an introduction to Sacred Scripture.
      These lead to a positive view of being human,
         to trust,
         to freedom,
         to self-giving,
         and to joyful participation in life.
Fourth, the family is the essential and first place
   where catechesis occurs,
   complemented by the school or religious education program.
[179] As young people enter school,
   parents, catechists, and school teachers
   should collaborate to use every suitable moment
      to lead the child to Christ.
[180] And when no Christian school is available,
   or when the family does not support a child's faith,
   the parish community has an obligation
      to assist that child to grow in faith.
This might be done by dialoguing with the family,
   by proposing various forms of catechesis,
   and by giving generous and loving support.

Catechesis of young people
[181] The first victims of the spiritual and cultural crisis
   gripping the world today
   are young people.
But, at the same time,
   society depends upon them for its future.
This fact stimulates us to assist young people
   to grow in their faith.
We speak of young people in three age groups:
   pre-adolescence,
   adolescence,
   and young adulthood.

The first of these is often overlooked
    but during this time of life
    confirmation is usually celebrated.
In many cases, from the moment of confirmation onward,
    young people abandon their faith,
        making confirmation more a "graduation"
        than an "initiation."
We must address this effectively,
    and at the same time
    also revitalize our ministries to them as they
        enter full adolescence and young adulthood.
[182] Young people live in a difficult age today
    and are victims of very rapid change
    and uncertain futures.
They are also in the process of self-discovery
    with its common sense of disenchantment,
        boredom,
        and personal crises.
Often during this time,
    young people feel alienated from the Church
    either due to a lack of family witness
    or poor catechesis in their youth.
But often, too, they desire more religious depth,
    more solidarity,
    and more commitment.
[183] In the gospel, young people speak directly to Christ
    who calls them to an enterprise
    of personal and community growth.
[184] Here are some general directions which emerge
    as we consider this.
First, remember than not all young people
    are in the same place
    with regard to religious faith.
Some are not even baptized
    or have not completed their initiation
    while others are moving towards a religious commitment
    or have already made such a commitment.

Second, the most successful catechesis
    will be laced into the very life situations
    of the young people themselves,
        taking into account their challenges,
        and employing them in their own formation.
Third, gathering young people in groups
    and offering them the chance for spiritual direction,
        are effective approaches.
[185] We should provide a "youth catechumenate"
    during school years whenever possible,
    as well as other forms of catechesis.
Involving young people in various activities
    which prepare them to grow in faith
    will animate the formation program
        and reach them where catechesis itself cannot.
The language we use in addressing young people
    is vitally important to consider.
The Church's jargon must be translated
    into their terms
    so they can meet Christ.

Catechesis for the aged
[186] Sometimes older members of the parish
    are forgotten when it comes to catechesis,
    as though they had received all they need
        earlier in life.
But catechesis is lifelong;
    it never ends.
In providing for older parish members
    we should take into account their situations,
    their sense of isolation,
    and the risk that they may feel marginalized.
The family plays a major role
    in catechizing the elderly,
    for here it takes place with acceptance and love.
The aged should participate fully
    in the catechetical enterprise of the total parish.

[187] In particular, older parish members
    often have a rich, solid faith,
    having lived their journey of faith
        with hope and thanksgiving.
Others may have lived with less faith
    and come now to be enriched in their final years.
And some may be profoundly wounded,
    even by the Church itself,
    and be in need of healing, forgiveness, and peace.
Whatever their situations,
    the condition of the aged calls for a catechesis of hope,
    derived from the certainty that they soon shall meet God.
[188] We also have in the aged members
    a fount of wisdom,
    as pictured in the Scriptures,
        making them "natural catechists"
        within the community.
Call on them to assist in passing on the faith
    which they have lived,
    and everyone will be enriched.
In this way, a fundamental dialogue between generations
    is promoted
    within both the family and the community.

Chapter Three

Catechesis for special situations, mentalities, and environments

The disabled and handicapped

[189] Those who suffer handicaps of any kind
    are considered particularly beloved
    by the Lord and the community.
Growth in our understanding of handicaps,
    along with progress in specialized pedagogy,
    makes it possible and desirable
        for all to have adequate catechesis.
If they're baptized, they have a right to catechesis,
    and if not, they're called to salvation.
In either case, the love of God for the weakest
    indicates their capability to grow in holiness.
Programs for catechesis should be personalized
    and should use modern pedagogical methods.
They should be in the mainstream of parish life.

The marginalized

[190] Here we speak of the immigrant,
    refugee,
    nomad,
    those who travel for work,
    the chronically ill,
    drug addicts,
    and prisoners.
The solemn word of Jesus
    is calling us to serve the least among us
    and assures us of the grace we need
        to serve these groups of people.
Certain catechists are called to serve the marginalized
    and should have the full support of the community.
Their approach to catechesis will differ from others
    but will have lasting effects.

Catechesis for different groups
[191] Some people, because of their professional training,
        require special catechetical attention.
These include workers,
        professionals,
        artists,
        scientists,
        and university students.
All of these demand an approach which employs
        their own language
        while maintaining fidelity to the message.

Environmental catechesis
[192] The service of the faith today
        is conscious of the environment where people live,
        both the rural and the urban.
The catechesis of country people will reflect
        needs experienced in the country,
                often linked with poverty and superstition.
But country life is also rich in simplicity,
        trust in life,
        a sense of solidarity with one's neighbor,
        faith in God,
        and fidelity to religion.
Urban catechists must take a wide variety of conditions
        into account in the city,
        including the range between rich and poor,
                stress in modern life,
                mobility,
                temptations to escapism and irresponsibility,
                oppressive anonymity,
                and loneliness.

Chapter Four

Catechesis in the socio-religious context

[193] Many people today live in situations
    where their faith is seriously challenged.
Unbelief and religious indifference are widespread.
    A purely secular view of life is common.
And in the face of such diversity,
    many Christians are confused or lost,
    not sure how to respond to what they see and hear.
Some abandon their faith
    while others water it down
    or others wander into false religions.
Therefore, it is necessary to nourish and sustain
    one's faith constantly.
[194] What is needed in these situations
    is a catechesis of evangelization,
        impregnated with the spirit of God
        and offered in language adapted to the times
        —and the hearers.
Such catechesis helps Christians know their identity
    as children of God
    open to dialogue with the world.
It stresses the fundamental elements of the faith
    and stimulates a real process of conversion.
It deepens the truth and value of the Christian message
    and helps them discern the gospel
    and live it in their everyday lives.
It enables them to be articulate in explaining their hope
    and encourages them to give witness to their faith.

Catechesis and popular devotion
[195] Popular devotion might be defined
    as an expression of the search for God
    which is full of fervor and purity.
Catechesis should offer wise direction to such devotion
    so that it does not lead to errors or fanaticism,

so that it avoids superstition,
     or religious ignorance.
For such devotion is based on love for God
    and a deep belief in God's compassion.
It can arouse in men and women
     virtue and strength,
     a sense of God's abiding presence,
     an ability to witness to the faith,
     and the strength to endure persecution.
Whatever its sort, popular devotion
     should always lead one to God in Jesus Christ.
[196] In particular, devotion to the Mother of God
     is often very strong.
In some cases, good catechesis is required
     in order to restore to these devotions
     elements which have become lost or obscure.
Marian devotion must always lead to Christ,
     must always celebrate the Trinity,
     and must always be set in the context of the Church.
Such devotions should be based on excellent Scripture scholarship,
     good liturgical principles,
     and sensitive ecumenical considerations.

Catechesis in the context of ecumenism
[197] Every Christian community is called
     to recognize its ecumenical vocation
     in whatever circumstance it finds itself.
Every community should engage in dialogue,
     and should initiate ways to increase Christian unity.
Catechesis, therefore,
     must also embrace an ecumenical dimension
     by adhering to the following:
First, the deposit of faith is guarded by the Catholic Church
     and should be treated comprehensively.
Second, catechesis should also make plain
     that unity which does exist in beliefs,
     why divisions do exist,
     and what is being done to overcome them.

Catechesis should also arouse a desire for unity
    and prepare young people to live with others
    by cultivating their own Catholic identity
    and a respect for the faith of others.
[198] Local bishops may undertake ecumenical initiatives
    where they deem them necessary,
    but a full Catholic catechesis must also be provided.
And Catholic schools where a diversity of faith is found
    can also be places for dialogue.

Catechesis in relationship to Judaism
[199] Whenever the Church delves into her own mystery,
    the story of salvation,
        we discover our links with the Jewish people,
        the first to hear the word of God.
In the very words of the document from Vatican II
    which addresses this,
"Religious instruction, catechesis, and preaching
    should not form only towards objectivity,
        justice,
        and tolerance
    but also in understanding and dialogue.
Both of our traditions are too closely related
    to be able to ignore each other.
It is necessary to encourage a reciprocal consciousness
    at all levels."
In particular an objective of catechesis
    should be to overcome every form
        of anti-semitism.

Catechesis in the context of other religions
[200] For the most part,
    Christians today live with many other religions
    sharing the same neighborhood and community.
In this context, especially with regard to Islam,
    catechesis assumes a delicate responsibility.
First, it must strengthen the faith of those
    who live in such multi-religious situations,
    especially when they're the minority.

Toward this end, we need solid, fervent communities,
    with native catechists.
Second, catechesis helps make Christians aware
    of their neighbors' beliefs,
        helping them see whatever is contrary to Christian faith,
            but also whatever is complementary.
And third, catechesis promotes a lively sense
    of reaching out to others,
        offering a witness of Christian faith and hope,
            mutual respect,
            understanding,
            and cooperation in defense of human rights,
                and the care of the poor.

Catechesis in relation to "new religious movements"
[201] There are many, many sects and cults
    which have arisen around the world today,
    too many to name or even categorize well.
Some are movements of Christian origin,
    while others derive from oriental religions
        or esoteric traditions.
Here again, Christian catechesis is very important
    in helping to deepen and confirm the faith,
    and it must be ongoing throughout life.
Christians must be helped to engage correctly with Scripture,
    to pray frequently,
    to avoid error,
    to understand their faith fully,
    and to avoid situations dangerous to their faith.
These movements do express a yearning for God
    and should be seen as a marketplace to be evangelized.
The Church has an immense heritage of faith
    to offer humankind,
    a heritage in Christ who called himself
        the way, the truth, and the life.

Chapter Five

Catechesis in the socio-cultural context

Catechesis and contemporary culture

[202] Catechesis is called to bring the power of the gospel
　　　into contemporary culture.
In this, catechesis is guided by "the rule of faith"
　　　which is illuminated by the Church's official teachings
　　　and further investigated by theology.
Since the earliest years of the Church
　　　when the gospel went out from Christ,
　　　it has always been implanted within a culture.
Indeed, faith lives in the hearts of women and men
　　　who live, always, within a specific culture.
For catechesis, this is a demanding and delicate art:
　　　to remain faithful to the message
　　　while allowing it to be heard within people's own cultures.
There is, indeed, a need for more reflection on this.

Duties of catechesis for inculturation of the faith

[203] First, to know in depth the culture of people
　　　and how deeply it is rooted in their lives.
Second, to see a cultural dimension in the gospel itself:
　　　on the one hand that it doesn't spring from human culture,
　　　and on the other that it can't be isolated from its original,
　　　　　first-century culture.
Third, to proclaim the profound conversion of culture
　　　which the power of the gospel brings about.
Fourth, to see how the gospel both transcends culture
　　　and is also found "planted" within every culture,
　　　　　even if not consciously.
Fifth, to promote the expression of the gospel
　　　in the very language of those
　　　　　who have been evangelized by it,
　　　while remaining faithful to our common faith language.
Sixth, to maintain the full content of the faith
　　　and explain doctrine completely

while taking into account the culture
in which it is being received.

Methodological processes
[204] Catechesis does not merely add the gospel
to a given culture as window dressing
but implants it deeply within the cultural setting,
interacting with local custom,
discerning God's presence there already,
naming sin for what it is,
and calling people to radical conversion to God,
while also allowing them to mature
in the faith.

The need for and criteria of evaluation
[205] When evaluating catechetical programs,
especially experimental ones,
watch for possible errors due to allowing
elements of other religions
to be mixed with ours.
What we wish to have instead is a catechesis
which inspires the intellect to accept the faith
and also touches one's heart and transforms one's conduct.
Catechesis in this latter case
bridges the gap between belief and life,
between the Christian message and the culture.
It leads to true holiness.

Those responsible for inculturation
[206] Inculturation must always be a reflection
of the life of the community
not merely a few leaders.
It must be entered into by all in the community:
clergy, pastoral workers, and laity.
[207] There are several moments when inculturation occurs.
The most apt moment is catechesis of the young
and adult catechesis
where faith and life are best correlated.

It also occurs in the Christian initiation of children
    where so much learning happens:
        motivation in life,
        education of conscience,
        familiarity with biblical and sacramental language,
        and a historical understanding.
A privileged means of this is the liturgy,
    especially the homily,
    the readings,
    and the flow of the liturgical year.
Also privileged are those moments when
    the care of the family occurs:
        marriages,
        funerals,
        visits to the sick,
        feasts of patron saints,
            and others.

Language and media
[208] Catechesis which truly implants the message
    in the culture where it is found
    must be thoughtful about the language
        used to witness and teach.
The language found in the creed and liturgy,
    as well as that in the dogmatic formulations
        of the Church
    should be respected.
But the meaning of these elements
    and their importance to life
    should be expressed in "local cultural language"
        as much as possible.
For example, the language of today's children and young people,
    that of academics and intellectuals,
    as well as that of the illiterate and simple,
    or that of the handicapped,
        all have their place in catechesis.
[209] A key connection is made between language,
    which we've just been discussing,

and the means of communication,
    otherwise called "media."
Here are some norms when using media in catechesis.
First, we should balance the media's language of the image
    with the word itself which is what is being taught.
Second, we should safeguard genuine religious meaning
    whenever using the media.
Third, we should promote in the audience
    an ability to grasp the deep meaning of what is presented.
And fourth, we should devise catechetical aids
    that meet these criteria and are effective.

[210] The *Catechism of the Catholic Church*
    calls for local catechisms
    that will attend to all the things
    we have said in this chapter.
[211] The gospel seeks a form of catechesis
    which reaches people wherever they live:
        in the family,
        at school or work,
        and during free time.
Catechesis must discern and penetrate
    these situations in life
    because this is where the culture
    has its greatest influence.
We hope to let the light of the gospel
    enlighten human progress in areas such as
        communications,
        civil campaigns for peace,
        the development and liberation of peoples,
        the protection of creation,
        the defense of human rights,
            especially minorities, women, and children,
        scientific research,
        and international relations.
[212] Judging what is present in any particular culture,
    and forming catechetical programs to address that,
    will lead to an effective witness of the faith,
        while respecting the local cultural setting.

84

There will be many ways this is done
    depending on the local situation.
Some nations are new to Christianity,
    while some need new evangelization.
In some places there is great pluralism and secularism,
    while in others this is not so.
In all catechetical programs,
    care must be taken to be certain
    that the local culture is addressed
        and the gospel made plain.
[213] We hope to see local Churches
    take up this campaign
    to properly inculturate the gospel,
    and develop their own standards,
        under the leadership of their bishops.
We hope to see training centers,
    new local directories,
    and catechetical texts.
[214] Local bishops should encourage growth
    in catechetical ministries.
First, they should promote catechesis
    to end religious ignorance.
Second, they should pilot
    experiments in inculturation
    especially in the Catechumenate.
Third, they should provide such catechetical support
    in all the languages found in the local culture.
And fourth, they should remain in dialogue
    with other local Churches and with the Holy See.

Part Five

Catechesis in the Particular Church

[215] We now turn our attention
    to how catechesis is done
    in particular local Churches.
[216] First we'll consider *who* does the work:
    clergy, religious, deacons, and laity.
Second, we'll analyze catechist formation.
Third, we'll consider *where* catechesis
    is best accomplished.
And finally, we'll consider organizational matters,
    relevant in all parts of the Church
    around the world.

Chapter One

The ministry of catechesis in the particular Churches and its agents

The particular Church

[217] The gospel is proclaimed and lived
in a particular local community or diocese
which is part of the universal Church.

[218] The two pillars on which the local Church is built
are the proclamation of the gospel
and the Eucharist.

Catechesis is part of the life of every local Church,
and by means of it
everyone who comes with a desire to know Christ
is provided with a formative process
that allows them to celebrate their faith
within a specific cultural setting.

Hence, everyone proclaims their faith in their own language,
just as at Pentecost.

[219] Here are some traits which are to be found
in every local Church's catechetical ministries.

First, catechesis is a unique ministry in the diocese
performed jointly by priests, deacons, religious, and laity
all in communion with the local bishop.

The entire community feels responsible for catechesis
which allows the word of God to be handed on
in a complete way.

Second, catechesis is always connected with a parish,
and is never a purely private activity.

Third, the task of the catechist as an educator in the faith
differs from all other ministries,
even when fully coordinated with them.

And fourth, other players than catechists
play a role in developing a fruitful program,
including those who form catechists,
those who prepare texts and other materials,
and those who organize and plan.

[220] Catechesis is a responsibility
of the entire Christian community
and should not be the work of catechists and priests alone.
Indeed, the entire community,
by the way it lives and acts and thinks,
is engaged in the catechetical process
whether it wants to be or not!
Newcomers to the community,
especially those in the catechumenate,
arrive to a rich mixture of relationships.
Just as immigrants shape the nation to which they go,
so newcomers to the Church shape us,
as do all those in catechesis.
[221] Not only does the community give to those being catechized,
it also receives much from them.
They bring new religious and human wealth
and add strength to the parish.
Thus, catechesis not only prepares the newcomers,
but also brings the community itself to maturity.
However, while it's true that the community has a role,
not everyone within the community has the vocation
of catechist.
The Church confers the delicate task of passing on the faith
within the community
—in collaboration with sponsors and family members—
only to those called to this ministry.

The role of bishops
[222] Vatican II named preaching the gospel
a key role of the bishop.
Missionary activity and programs of catechesis
are two aspects of the bishop's ministry.
[223] The bishop, therefore, should assume
overall responsibility for catechesis.
This implies, among other things:
First, that he make catechesis a priority
by providing the personnel and money for it.

Second, that he show solicitude for catechesis
by watching carefully over it.
Third, that he bring about a real passion
for catechesis in his diocese
that will touch all those involved in it.
Fourth, that he ensure proper formation of catechists,
both in their knowledge of the faith
and in their skills and methods.
And fifth, that he establish a well-planned program
in his diocese,
connected to his overall pastoral plan
and coordinated with the local episcopal conference.

The role of priests
[224] The role of the priest in catechesis
arises from his ordination.
He is commissioned to form the community,
coordinate its services,
and call forth its charisms.
The priest is the "educator of the faith"
and must work to see to it
that all the faithful are offered catechesis.
However, the priest is also at the service
of the "common priesthood of the faithful"
and therefore, must call forth and support catechists,
who are also called by God to this work.
Thus the priest accomplishes what Vatican II hoped they would:
"to recognize and promote the dignity of the laity,
and their specific role in the Church's mission."
[225] Specifically, this means the priest must:
First, foster a sense of common responsibility for catechesis
within his parish.
Second, care for the basic formation
which catechists need to do their work.
Third, promote a sense of vocation to catechetics
on the part of those who come forth.
Fourth, integrate catechesis into the whole life of the community,
and foster the link between catechesis and liturgy.

And finally, to connect their parish programs
    with the diocesan pastoral program.
Experience teaches that the quality of a parish program
    depends, in large part,
        on the commitment of the priest.

The role of parents
[226] The witness of Christian life
    given by parents in the family
    comes to children with tenderness and respect.
Thus, children grow up living in the closeness of love—
    which is the closeness of God and Jesus—
    made plain by their parents.
This leaves its mark for the rest of their lives!
The childhood religious awakening
    which takes place in the family
    is simply irreplaceable.
It is most powerful when parents take the time
    to explain to their children
    the religious significance or meaning
        of certain events
            including holy days and family moments,
        and of social, political, or moral questions.
And this is made even more powerful
    when parents connect it to the methodical catechesis
    their children receive in the parish program.
Indeed, we might say that "family catechesis
    precedes,...accompanies, and enriches all forms of catechesis."
[227] In the sacrament of matrimony,
    parents receive the grace and the ministry
        of the Christian education of their children.
This educational activity,
    which is both human and religious,
    is a true ministry through which the gospel is proclaimed
        and family life is transformed
            into a journey of faith.
The Christian community must, therefore, help parents
    by whatever means work best,

to prepare for and assume their responsibility—
    which is especially delicate today—
    of educating their children in the faith.

The role of religious

[228] Those called to religious life
    have a special role to play in catechetics.
The Church hopes they will dedicate themselves
    to this ministry.
Their particular contribution to catechesis
    can never be substituted for by priests or laity.
This is because, by their public witness to faith
    founded on their vowed life,
    they are a living sign of Christ's way of life.
In short, they are a sign of the kingdom of God.
[229] Many religious institutes were founded
    for the purpose of Christian education.
Over the years their contributions have shaped
    the Church's educational ministry
    as each community's unique charism was exercised.

The role of lay catechists

[230] The laity, too, have a significant role to play
    in the Church's mission of catechesis.
They bring their own gifts,
    inserted as they are in the affairs of the world.
Because they share the same lifestyle
    as those they catechize,
    lay catechists are effective in helping people
        see how the gospel
        is lived out in everyday life.
Indeed, lay catechists are a model for those being catechized.
[231] The vocation to catechesis springs from baptism
    and is strengthened by confirmation.
Hence, laypeople participate in the priestly,
    kingly,
    and prophetic ministry of Christ.

From a loving knowledge of Christ,
>   laypeople desire to proclaim him
>   and lead others to know him.
To be called to this ministry,
>   affirmed by the Church for it,
>   and dedicated to it,
>   is a high calling!
Regardless of the amount of time one can commit,
>   the work of catechesis is a worthy ministry.
There should be some persons in each parish and diocese
>   who are committed to it full time, however,
>   to strengthen local programs.

Types of catechists
[232] There are various types of catechists in the Church.
First, there are those in missionary countries
>   who have specific responsibility for catechesis.
Second, there are those deprived of the constant presence
>   of a priest,
>   especially in rural areas around the world,
>   where the catechist animates the local Church.
Third, there are those working where "new evangelization"
>   is needed for both young people and adults.
Fourth, there are those working specifically
>   with children and adolescents,
>   especially if family participation is inadequate.
Fifth, there are those working with adults
>   during the time their children are in formation
>   for baptism or First Communion,
>   or as they prepare for their own marriage.
Sixth, there are those working in delicate situations,
>   such as with the aging,
>   with the handicapped or disabled,
>   with migrant workers,
>   or with those marginalized or rejected by society.
And there may be other kinds of catechists needed as well
>   depending on the needs of the local Church.

Chapter Two

Formation for the service of catechesis

Pastoral care of catechists in a particular Church

[233] The pastoral care of catechists is essential
and, toward that end, we now list several elements of it.

First, in parish life we should think about catechesis
as a vocation
and about the need for specialized catechists.

Second, this new way of thinking will result
in having a number of full-time catechists,
in addition to part-time catechists who are more numerous.
The full-time catechists will provide stability
and professionalism.

Third, parishes should organize a more balanced distribution
of catechists among the various groups of the parish,
studying the needs of adult catechesis
and that of children.

Fourth, we want to foster
what we call "animators of catechetical activity"
at the diocesan, regional, and parish level.

Fifth, we encourage an adequate formation program
for catechists
both for basic training
and continuing education.

Sixth, parishes should attend to the personal spiritual needs of catechists,
both individually and as a group,
which is fundamentally the job of the local pastor.

And seventh, to enter into a sort of "total parish catechesis,"
coordinating carefully among the pastoral ministries
so that catechesis is not isolated.

[234] Diocesan pastoral programs must give absolute priority
to the formation of lay catechists;
pastors, too, must be well-trained in catechesis.

This ministry in the Church will not be effective
unless and until this step is taken.

We consider it of utmost importance here.

[235] The formation of catechists will prepare them
	to share their own faith in Jesus
	and lead others to entrust themselves to Jesus.
The absolute summit and center of catechetical formation
	lies in learning how to communicate
		the gospel message effectively.
Jesus Christ is the center of this.
It is Christ whom we communicate to others,
		and the catechist must be able to animate the journey to Christ
			which those in his or her care are making.
Toward this end, then,
		the catechist will be prepared to proclaim Christ,
		the first step,
			but also to make known the story of Christ
			as a story of salvation.
The catechist will also lead those being catechized
		to know Jesus Christ as the Son of God
		and to desire the union with Christ
			which the sacraments of initiation celebrate.
All the rest of catechesis is a deepening of this first journey.
[236] Because the catechist makes Christ known
		within the context of the Church
		the formation of the catechist also occurs
			within that context.
In short, this means that the catechist, through formation,
		enters into deep communion with the Church
		and faithfully passes on the faith
			while adapting it to cultures, ages, and situations.

The criteria for the formation of catechists
[237] The following factors should be taken into account
		when the formation of catechists is being done.
First, catechists must work in the present moment in history,
		with its values, challenges, and disappointments.
			Therefore, they must have deep faith,
			an abiding love for the Church,
			and a great social sensitivity.
Second, the concept of catechesis which the Church holds
		must be part of formation.

It's not merely a matter of teaching
but also of witnessing to faith
and leading learners to initiation.
Third, catechists might be tempted to share their opinions
about the Church and its situation in today's world
but catechesis requires that they be formed
to link the truth and meaning of the Church's teachings
with its practices and doctrines,
all personal opinions aside.
Fourth, lay catechists must be formed to understand
that their vocation arises from their own baptism,
not from the vocations of the priests and religious
alongside whom they serve.
And finally, the method used to train catechists
should resemble closely that which the catechists
will use in their work.
Hence they learn a method for their own use
even as they're being trained.
[238] The deepest dimension of catechist formation
deals with the very person of the catechist,
his or her very being.
One's being, both human and Christian,
is formed when one matures as a person,
as a believer,
and as an apostle.
The catechist in this process is committed
both to the message of Christ
and to the human family.
Knowing well that message,
and knowing well what it means to be human
with all its joys, hopes, dreams, and challenges—
this is the field of the catechist.
Expertise in this field makes the catechist great.
Formation must move in this direction.
[239] By engaging in catechetical work,
the catechist also grows in maturity,
becoming more able to relate,
promote dialogue,

work in groups,
and witness to the faith.
Indeed, the catechetical activity in which one engages
springs from the center of one's life,
deepening spirituality for all.
Indeed, catechists catechize others
by first catechizing themselves!
By having the zeal for the reign of God
which Jesus possessed,
the catechist grows and matures constantly
in his or her apostolic vocation.
[240] Besides being a witness,
which we've just discussed,
a catechist is also a teacher,
providing a comprehensive, living,
and complete education in the mystery of the faith.
This includes, first, the three great eras of God's action in
human history:
the Old Testament period,
the life of Christ,
and the history of the Church.
This also includes the center of the Christian message:
the Creed,
the liturgy,
the moral life,
and prayer.
Sacred Scripture is the soul of catechist formation,
and the *Catechism of the Catholic Church* is its reference point.
[241] This combination of biblical and theological formation
has the following qualities:
First, it should be of a summary nature,
honoring the "hierarchy of truths"
and presented in an orderly fashion.
Second, the formation offered should assist the catechist
to articulate his or her faith
in light of today's needs and social situations.
(There is, indeed, a need for all the lay faithful
to be articulate in this way.)

Third, it must be a theological training
    that connects to everyday life
    both to inspire it and to judge it
        in light of the gospel.
And finally, catechist formation should enable catechists
    to communicate effectively
    but also *to be heard by those being catechized.*
[242] Beyond theology,
    catechists should also be trained in the fields
        of psychology and sociology.
By understanding what motivates human persons,
    how personality is structured,
    the deep needs and desires of the human heart,
    the phases of the human life cycle,
    and that which opens humans to the sacred,
        a catechist will be more effective.
Likewise, by understanding culture more deeply,
    as well as the nature of religious experience,
    economic conditions,
    good educational methods,
    and communications skills,
        a catechist will also be more effective.
[243] In forming catechists,
    theology and these human sciences
    should work hand-in-glove.
[244] Over and above developing the person of the catechist,
    and his or her knowledge of faith and human science,
    formation should also cultivate *technique.*
God sows faith in the heart of the human person
    and the catechist must cultivate this
    in today's world and culture
        by being attentive to people,
    by organizing learning activities,
    and by leading a group toward maturity.
Catechists must adapt the general principles of catechesis
    to their own personalities and styles.
[245] It is never enough for a catechist
    simply to follow the notes in the text.

These notes and teaching methods must always
    be creatively adapted to the catechist's own style.
In this way, those to be catechized will be animated
    by their relationship with the catechist,
    by the technique being used,
    and by the content of the material itself.
[246] Catechetical ministry always occurs within a community.
[247] Here are some ways a parish can help form catechists:
First, it can keep alive the sense
    that its catechists are *sent* by the parish.
Second, it can provide formal catechetical training.
Third, it can provide preparation for the immediate tasks
    by a group process accompanied by an evaluation.
And fourth, it can provide continuing education
    throughout the year
    connected to the liturgical seasons.
[248] And finally, schools for catechists
    can provide the in-depth formation that is needed.
[249] For "ordinary catechists,"
    those who teach week in and week out,
    a systematic, unfolding process of formation
        will assure quality and self-identity.
By meeting catechists from other parishes
    Church unity is promoted,
    and everyone gains from that.
[250] For "catechetical leaders"
    catechetical institutes are needed
    either within a diocese or among nearby dioceses.
Such institutes offer a more demanding course,
    and can be combined with training
    for other pastoral ministries,
        tailored to meet local needs.
[251] For "experts in catechesis"
    university level programs are needed
    either nationally or internationally.
Such programs should also engage in catechetical research.
[252] More wealthy Churches
    should assist those with fewer means
    to afford catechetical training at all levels.

Chapter Three

[253] There are specific places
    where initiatory catechesis
    and continuing education in the faith occur.
The "community" has been the place where
    faith is realized and lived, including
        the family,
        the parish,
        Catholic schools,
        Christian associations and movements,
        and basic ecclesial communities.
[254] Catechesis doesn't change really,
    but it is realized in these various places
    and is always rooted in community.
The community, therefore, plays a significant role
    in the catechetical enterprise of the Church.
Within the community, catechesis occurs in various places;
    we now present a list of them.

The family as the environment in which faith grows
[255] Parents are the primary educators
    in the faith.
Together with them,
    especially in some cultures,
    all the members of the family
        also play a role
        in the formation of young members.
The family is defined by Vatican II
    as a *domestic Church*
    which means that every family
        embodies the different parts of the Church
            within itself.
One part of this is a sense of reaching out to others,
    known in the Church as "mission."
Another part is the desire to teach about the faith itself,
    known in the Church as "catechesis."

Yet another part is prayer within the family,
    the practice of charity,
    a welcoming front door,
    and a place of refuge from the demands of the world.
The family passes on human values
    in the Christian tradition,
    and it awakens a sense of God in its young members.
It teaches the first tentative steps of prayer,
    it forms the moral conscience,
    and it teaches human love
        as a reflection of divine love.
Indeed, catechesis in the home
    is more witness than teaching,
    more occasional than systematic,
    and more daily than structured into periods.
In the family, the role of grandparents is increasing,
    along with homespun wisdom
    and a Christian climate of life.

The baptismal catechumenate for adults
[256] Another place where catechesis occurs
    is, of course,
    in the baptismal catechumenate.
The catechumenate has been instituted by the Church
    as the means by which adults who so desire
    are prepared to receive the sacraments of initiation
        at the Easter Vigil.
In the catechumenate,
    catechesis is linked to the community;
    the Church, you might say, *surrounds* the catechumens,
        showing them by example
            what it means to belong to the community of Christ.

The parish
[257] The parish community is the most important place
    where formation occurs.
This is where people become aware of themselves
    as the community of God,
    a welcoming and warm home.

Here is where faith is born and nourished.
Because of urbanization today,
      the parish is undergoing immense change,
      but it remains the focus of faith for many,
            even for those who are non-practicing.
It is also the prime place where catechesis occurs.

[258] Here are the conditions that must be fulfilled
      in order for the parish to succeed
      in its ministry of catechesis.
First, adult catechesis must be given priority.
      By this we mean a *post*-baptismal catechesis
      in the form of the catechumenate,
            through which adults can grow and mature
            in their faith.
Second, we must announce the Good News
      to those who are alienated
      or indifferent about their faith.
      Pre-sacramental meetings are fundamental for this.
Third, the development of small ecclesial communities
      can be of great assistance in catechesis.
And finally, while the first three points here deal with adults,
      the catechesis of children and young people
      also remains a necessary element.

Catholic schools
[259] Another significant place where catechesis occurs
      is the Catholic school.
Vatican II helped change our thinking about schools,
      moving from considering them an institution
      to considering them a *community*.
The school should be animated by a spirit of charity and liberty;
      it should assist the young to grow
            in the new life of their baptism;
      and it should help them see the world
            through the eyes of Christ.
The mission of the school is accomplished within its community,
      which includes teachers, administrators, and parents

(who are the first educators of their children),
as well as the students themselves!
[260] When parents send their children to Catholic schools
because of their connection to the Church,
catechesis and religious instruction are paramount.
When they send their children to Catholic schools
because of their high quality educational offerings,
catechetical activity is more limited.
Local bishops' conferences should specify
the kind of catechetics to be implemented in their schools.

Associations and movements
[261] Associations and movements of the faithful
exist to help the disciples of Jesus
live their faith more fully.
[262] In all such organizations, it's necessary to provide
some level of catechetical training and formation.
When doing so, here are some guidelines.
First, the catechesis in this context
should employ word, memory, and witness
(doctrine, celebration, and commitment in life)
as its primary means.
Second, even though such movements tend to have
their own unique spirituality,
it's necessary to educate in what is common
to all members of the Church
before educating in that which is unique to these movements.
Third, such movements are not alternatives
to parish-based catechesis.

Basic ecclesial communities
[263] Small communities of the faithful have emerged
because people want to live their faith more fully.
Large parishes simply cannot provide the environment
for most people to do that.
These communities are a sign of the Church's vitality.
They are a place where people gather
and where their faith is truly deepened,
but also where friendships emerge,

as does personal recognition,
a spirit of shared responsibility,
vocational response,
and concern for the problems of the world.
To be authentic, all such communities must be in union
with the Church's pastors
and be committed to outreach.
[264] In these communities, an enriching catechesis
can occur.
When it does, it should be faithful to the larger Church,
deepen the life of the greater community,
and be a place of welcome for those making
the catechetical journey.

Chapter Four

The organization of catechetical pastoral care in particular Churches

[265] The diocesan catechetical office,
    under the management of the bishop,
    directs and moderates all catechetical activity.
[266] The diocesan office does the following:
First, it analyzes the state of catechetics in the diocese,
    taking the real needs of the diocese into account.
Second, it develops a plan of action.
Third, it promotes formation of catechists.
Fourth, it screens the materials to be used
    by parish programs,
    including catechisms, programs, and guides.
Fifth, it fosters diocesan movements
    such as the catechumenate,
    and parish-level catechetical programs.
Sixth, it seeks to constantly improve
    both personnel and the materials used in the diocese.
Seventh, it collaborates with the liturgical office,
    given the close connection between the two.
[267] To accomplish this, the diocesan office
    should employ people who hold specific competencies
    and the work should be divided accordingly.

Interdiocesan cooperation
[268] Wherever possible and helpful,
    dioceses should share resources and combine actions
    to be more powerfully effective.

The episcopal conference
[269] The national episcopal conference
    should establish a catechetical office
    to assist various dioceses with their work.
Such an office has two functions:
    To oversee publications,
        national meetings,

relations with the media,
and other tasks beyond the means of any one diocese.
And to assist dioceses that are not as well-provided
with catechetical materials.
It might also work internationally,
if the local bishops deem it useful.

The Holy See
[270] The pope has a basic responsibility
to hand on the faith.
He acts through the Congregation for Clergy
to direct catechesis throughout the world.
[271] The Congregation, for its part,
promotes religious education of all Christians,
issues norms for catechetical programs,
maintains a watchful attention to such programs,
approves catechisms and other materials,
and assists local conferences or dioceses as needed.

Coordinating catechesis
[272] The local Church must coordinate catechesis
to ensure unity of faith
which is the basis of the Church's life.
[273] We will now consider this under three forms.
[274] The diocesan catechetical program
coordinates and unifies parish programs
which should provide at least these two services:
programs for children and young people
and programs for adults
—both flowing to and from
the sacraments of initiation.
In many places there is also need for such programs
for those in the last stages of their lives.
[275] Within any given parish,
these two programs (for children and for adults)
should be well-coordinated,
but the catechesis of adults is primary
and all the rest is organized around it.

People who are well-rounded in the faith may not need
> to enter a catechetical program,
> but may need instead other more solid nourishment.

[276] Here is the catechetical process:
> initial missionary proclamation
> followed by catechesis to deepen one's commitment,
> and then pastoral care beyond that for the rest of life.

But sometimes, in a given parish,
> it isn't that simple.

Ordinary catechesis, for example, is often offered
> to young people
> who need first to hear the proclamation
> and experience conversion.

Or parents of children in catechetical programs
> may not themselves be formed.

Or adult catechetical programs may be offered
> when what is needed is a program of conversion.

[277] So the current situation in the Church
> calls for well-coordinated programs,
> where all these elements are provided as needed.

[278] Each parish should take care to ensure
> that all aspects of formation are provided,
> and that all stages of growth in faith are supported
> by a unified and faithful inspiration.

The bottom line is that those called to faith in Christ
> make the same profession of faith,
> the same commitment to live as Jesus teaches.

Responsibilities of the catechetical ministry

[279] Each parish should be certain to have
> a realistic analysis of its catechetical context.

Specifically, how is catechesis situated
> in the process of evangelization,
> how is it balanced among age groups,
> how is it coordinated with the families,
> what is its internal quality,
> and how well are catechists formed?

Also, what human experiences have led people
    to be open to the mysteries of faith?
And in what concrete ways do people
    communicate with God?
In what moral situation do people live?
    What values emerge?
    And what counter-values are evident?
Finally, what is the cultural setting
    in which people live?
[280] Given the situations in which people find themselves,
    pastoral workers in catechesis
    should be open to the unfolding presence of God
        in people's lives.

[281] Once the catechetical context has been analyzed,
    a program of action must be formed.
Such a program must both address the local needs and realities
    and follow the norms of the universal Church.
Such programs are usually laid out for a year or so,
    after which they are evaluated and revised.
Realism should be the first characteristic
    of a program of action,
        then *simplicity, conciseness,* and *clarity.*
[282] Many national episcopal conferences
    establish guidelines for such programs.

Teaching tools
[283] Once the situation is correctly analyzed,
    the plan of action is determined,
    and the local bishops' guidelines followed,
        there comes the need to choose materials.
These include *textbooks*
    guides for teachers,
    and *audiovisual aids.*
Such tools must be
    linked with the real life of the generation
        to which they're addressed,
    able to speak the language of that generation,
    and aim to give those who use them a better grasp

of the mysteries of Christ
and a true conversion to God's will.

Local catechisms
[284] Local bishops are urged to prepare catechisms
that are both faithful to the *Catechism of the Catholic Church*
and in accord with the norms of this *Directory*.
Such catechisms are the best way to guide
parish catechetical work.
[285] The Holy See must approve all local catechisms
as a sign to the world of our unity
and to ensure faithful inculturation.

Conclusion

[286] In formulating these guidelines,
    every effort has been made to ensure
    that they're based on Vatican II
    and post-conciliar teachings of the Church.
We have also paid attention to the life of the Church
    as it is unfolding today.
[287] This directory is offered to the Church's pastors
    and their colleagues in ministry,
    to foster growth in their work
        and offer them hope.
[288] The effectiveness of catechesis, however,
    is always a gift from God.
None of what we do is possible without God's power
    and grace.
The silent and unseen action of the Holy Spirit
    can never be replaced with techniques,
        no matter how clever.
[289] May patience and trust abide
    in the spirituality of the catechist,
    since it is God who sows,
        gives growth,
        and brings to fruition the seed of God's word,
            planted in good soil
            and tended with love.
We recall here again that parable in Mark's gospel,
    showing the constant development of the seed:
"The kingdom of God," the text tells us,
    "is as if a man should scatter seed upon the ground,
    and should sleep and rise night and day,
    and the seed should sprout and grow,
        he knows not how.
The earth produces of itself first the blade,
    then the ear,
    then the full grain in the ear.

But when the grain is ripe,
>at once he puts in the sickle,
>because the harvest has come." (Mk 4:26–29)

[290] The Church invites the Spirit of the Father
>and of the Son
>to give life and fruitfulness to this ministry.

[291] We turn as well to the Blessed Virgin Mary
>who saw her own Son grow
>"in wisdom, age and grace."
>>May her example be ours,
>>and may her faith inspire us all.

Pope John Paul II approved the official translation
>of this document on August 11, 1997,
>and authorized its publication.